Walking with Paddy

Walking through the year with my four-legged friend

Copyright © 2023 Josephine Cullum-Fernandez

DEDICATION

For my daughter, Evelyn.

I hope time spent in nature brings you as much
happiness as it does me.

CONTENTS

A NOTE FROM THE AUTHOR

My aim with this book was to document my walks with Paddy for a whole year as a means of recording how our surroundings change through the seasons and the joyous moments shared with my four-legged best friend. I therefore chose to write up a few of our walks for each month of the year.

Whilst the original purpose of the book was for my personal interest, once I got writing I realised that my words may be enjoyed by others and thus self-publishing became a goal. So here I am, inviting you into the peace and quiet of my little patch of the Kentish countryside and I hope it brings you some escapism and inspiration to get outside and more connected to nature yourself. You will also find some of my trusty seasonal recipes amongst the stories- you're welcome.

Ready for an adventure? Grab your wellies and let's go walking!...

JANUARY

FRIDAY 8TH JANUARY 2021
8AM : MINUS 1 DEGREE C.

It's very cold this morning- below freezing- so I'm in need of all the layers! I've even found a pair of gloves with no holes in- result! I let Paddy out the door and he races to the end of the garden to rid us of the threat of an imposing magpie. He's full of it this morning. I think the frost has made him giddy.

Today we're doing the 'airport walk'- always reliable for seeing a good sunrise. We make our way over and, as we reach the play park, Paddy stops for his morning poo (always in the same spot). As I'm bending down to pick it up he ceremoniously kicks up the ground with his back feet, sending a barrage of frost right at my face- "Thanks, Pads!".

Once we reach the open fields I let Paddy off the lead. He bounds off and then picks up speed following the excitement of his feet breaking through icy puddles and the frosty grass brushing his legs. I, meanwhile, reach for my phone in an attempt to capture the beautiful sunrise. It's strikingly orange and gold in front of my eyes, yet on the phone screen it's dull and rather uninspiring. A phone will never do it justice.

It's silent as we walk, aside from our footsteps on the hard ground and the "swish" of my coat and waterproof trousers. The frozen puddles are just too tempting and I break through each one with the heel of my welly, relishing in the satisfying "crack" that results. It must have been a very cold night as the ice is thick, making a deep, hollow sound as I break through it and there is no water underneath, it's all frozen.

As I look up from the shards of ice surrounding my wellies I notice that something has caught Paddy's attention on the river bank. All becomes clear as he then comes rushing out, proudly displaying his prize. It's the large bit of plastic pipe we first found several weeks ago. He's delighted to have rediscovered it and proceeds to wrestle with it, dig at it with his paws and prance around with it. Not content to play alone, he now rushes towards me with it, dropping it at my feet to allow me to throw it for him. Before I know it, he's back again but now he's thrashing the pipe around, battering me with it in the process. He's such a thug. A loveable thug, but a thug nonetheless. My attempts to ignore him eventually work and, after some more solo-play, Paddy remembers there are potatoes in this field which he's very much partial to...

We've reached the turnaround point where Paddy feasts on rabbit poo, much to my disapproval, and now we're heading back. On the big wooden bridge I stop half way and watch Paddy in the river below me, tentatively taking a drink from the cold water. As I stand there, my eyes catch the frost on the top of the wooden barrier. It's beautiful and delicate and I suddenly feel a child-like urge to touch it with my tongue. It's cold and soft and I giggle at myself for what I've just done but there's nobody else here to witness it and Paddy doesn't judge so we just continue on.

I take a few more photos, this time with more success than trying to capture the sunrise. A close up of the frost on the footpath sign; an icy puddle and Paddy waiting patiently to cross the silvery railway track. It's all of these seemingly insignificant little things that actually provide so much wonder and joy if only we stop to notice them.

TUESDAY 12TH JANUARY 2021
7:50AM : 9 DEGREES C.

It's the kind of morning where all those "Lovely weather for ducks!" comments come out when passing other dog walkers. I simply plump for a stating-the-obvious "It's not very nice is it?". To be honest though, I don't really mind. I mean, it's not my weather of choice but I've got my waterproof coat, waterproof trousers, wellies and warm, woolly gloves on so I'm warm and dry (on the inside).

We've passed the cricket ground, navigated the rapidly growing puddles on the rough track and are making our way down the narrow footpath which passes the lake. I notice how sad everything looks on this grey day. The trees are still bare and most of the hawthorn berries are gone. But then a flash of yellow comes into view, that real 'sunshine' yellow. It's gorse flowers. There aren't many there but enough to bring a smile to my face when I think of the beautiful coconut-y aroma those bushes will emit when they're basked in sunshine in a few months' time. When that time comes I will stop to take a deep inhale of that gorgeous scent every time I pass it, just as I did last year.

At the end of the narrow path, Paddy is waiting patiently for me to give the "Okay" for his usual bolt through the small gap whilst I climb over the style. Today, however, there are sheep in the field so I clip Paddy's lead on. The combination of the rain and the sheep has really churned up the field. There are deep tyre tracks left by the farmer checking his flock in his 4x4 too. We trudge our way across the field, slipping, sliding and squelching as we go. We reach the gate on the far side and the clang of metal as I close it behind us usually causes the farm dog, Jessie, to commence her barking routine and come rushing out to see us. Today there is silence and I like to think it's because she's curled up, warm and dry in front of the agar.

We pass the barn in which as many of the cows as can fit are munching their way through their breakfast. The unlucky ones huddle together outside, using the side of the barn to shelter from the worst of the rain but still look pretty unhappy. As we walk past, Paddy eyes the cows whose size is somewhat intimidating, the cows eye Paddy with curiosity and I am happy to call out a "Morning moo cows!" to them, comforted by the strong metal bars separating us from them.

Up ahead, I notice a load of soldiers coming our way. We live near an army barracks so this isn't as bizarre as it might sound. However, it is quite unusual to see a whole squadron (is that the collective noun for a group of soldiers?) together. They are lined up, two by two, snaking their way towards us on the winding path like a centipede, all dressed in brown camo gear. When I first spotted them they were marching but now, after a shouted order from who I assume is the sergeant, they have picked up the pace to a jog. This increased movement and the sound of stomping boots and heavy bags bouncing on the soldiers' backs has piqued Paddy's interest. Ears up, tail up and slightly raised hackles, he stretches his neck as far as possible to try to find out what this strange thing coming towards us is. In an attempt to not get trampled I move into the long grass at the edge of the path and position myself between Paddy and the oncoming centipede. Thankfully the sergeant has the sense to order a return to their original pace before reaching us and Paddy just looks at them with a mixture of interest and suspicion as all twenty or so soldiers march past us.

The rest of our walk seems rather dull after this exciting encounter...

THURSDAY 21ST JANUARY 2021
7:30AM : 7 DEGREES C.

As we head outside I'm immediately grateful for the knitted headband protecting my ears from the harsh wind. There is evidence that it's been gusty overnight- a solitary Coke can in an otherwise tidy and perfectly manicured garden; a dustbin looking out of place on its side whilst its purple-lidded counterpart stands upright beside it; and a small tree now preventing passage through a narrow lane.

We head out into the field where Paddy, now unleashed, darts from hedgerow to clump of mud to tuft of grass to catch up on all of the scents which have accumulated since the last time we walked this way. Above us, the sky is alive with sea birds, presumably staying slightly in-land to avoid the stronger winds undoubtedly battering the coast. There must be well over one hundred and fifty of them.

A thick wall of cloud surrounds us, almost like we're in a coliseum, but above us there is blue sky. Although the cloud wall is grey, the very top edges of some patches are revealing a beautiful pink hew. The sun is rising, just like every other morning, but today the only evidence of it is in this slightly pink border to the top of the cloud wall.

I'm still marvelling at the clouds when into my eye line appears a gaggle of five or six geese flying overhead. I watch on as they flap their wings yet seem to make little headway. I assume they are aiming to join the rest of the geese which are all safely at ground level, mooching about in the grass. Determinedly, the geese push on and eventually execute a safe landing, despite the wind disrupting their course. Shortly behind the geese there is a lone heron. They always look so prehistoric to me, like a long-lost cousin of the Pterodactyl. I'm not sure where he's headed but he's having a similarly tough time.

As we cross over the bridge I notice how high the water level in the river is, although we seem to have got off lightly here as other parts of the country are currently facing severe flooding. I appreciate the gentle flow of water which is clear enough to reveal the plant life below. Across the bridge we walk beside the hedgerow where I keep my eyes trained firmly on the ground. The edge of this field is littered with rabbit holes and I've come a cropper on more than one occasion! Thankfully, I've now learnt where the deepest holes are but the long grass does a good job of obscuring them so I'm being cautious. When I reach more stable ground I look up and catch sight of a rabbit hopping across the pebbles towards the gorse up ahead. I smile because it's not just an ordinary rabbit but the beautiful light beige/ginger one which I've seen in this location a few times. Paddy spots her too and sprints off but, by the time he reaches the pebbles, she's already under the cover of the thick gorse.

We start to head back the way we came but it's more challenging now because, in addition to the slippery mud underfoot, we're now walking against the wind. It's so open and exposed here, devoid even of any tall trees or buildings close by, so we are battered by the wind and it feels like a full body workout to reach the relative protection of the first close of houses.

We're now just five minutes from home, walking along the pavement, when I feel the warm glow of the sun on my right cheek. I turn to see that the sun has been triumphant in rising above the wall of cloud. Paddy stops to sniff the grass and, behind him, I spot a big clump of narcissi- tall, strong and bright yellow, all in full bloom. In that moment, admiring the cheery flowers with the sun on my face, I trick myself into believing it is Spring.

SUNDAY 31ST JANUARY 2021
3PM : 6 DEGREES C.

I'm feeling that familiar slightly-too-full-but-incredibly-content feeling that so often comes after a good Sunday dinner and a glass of red wine. Now to leave the warmth of home and head out into the grey and mist which this final day of January has brought. I don my waterproofs and gloves, clip Paddy into his harness and off we go.

Upon reaching the cricket ground I'm pleased to see it is deserted, except for one solitary car in the car park. The lights are on and the engine is running so, at first, I think they are about to leave. However, a few minutes later, I come to the conclusion that the car's occupants are simply making the most of the heater before embarking on a lap of the field in the drizzle.

I've unleashed Paddy now and he's happily trotting along, frequently changing direction as new scents catch his attention and warrant further investigation. Once I'm confident he really is scenting the movements of other dogs and people, rather than sampling the ubiquitous rabbit droppings, I make my way over to the fence at the top of the field. On the other side of this fence is a flock of sheep but one in particular has caught my eye and I'm drawn to her. She had her head through the fence, eagerly munching on the grass which is clearly more tasty than that on her own side (the grass is always greener…), but now that I'm approaching she has taken a few steps back. We stand and look at each other for a few minutes and I compliment her on her beautiful fleece. It is incredibly long yet in very good condition, especially in light of the current mud, rain and wind. Her face looks so soft and almost fluffy. I notice a few other sheep behind her and can't help thinking they look comparatively ugly. Then I mentally chastise myself for this unkind thought and smile at them all before checking back on what Paddy is up to. I think he had noticed my pre-occupation with the sheep and took advantage of this as he is now most definitely chowing down on rabbit droppings like a kid with a bowl full of Nesquik! Knowing I'm now on to him, he saunters off and we move down the field until we reach the riverbank.

Here, Paddy surveys the rabbit holes and then picks up where he left off a few days ago with digging. I allow him five minutes of this natural behaviour which brings him so much joy. His tail is flicking to and fro as his front paws work hard, dragging back the dirt between his two back legs which are spread firmly behind. With earth being scattered around me and occasional squeaks of excitement as Paddy believes he's close to something this time, I look across the river and into the distance several fields away, I notice the familiar 4x4 of the local farmer slowly driving along a track. Farming is such a relentless profession. Every day is a work day for them, in all weathers too. My eyes pan around further and land on a solitary person in the lane. I had seen them walking along the lane as we entered the cricket ground but now they have come to a stop on the bend. After a moment I notice the person throwing something into the field. How strange. But, yes, again- several times in fact, I watch them pull their arm back and launch something into the field. I can't see what they're throwing or any indication as to why they might be doing this. An approaching car then seemingly interrupts this person's odd behaviour and my gaze leaves them.

It is starting to drizzle more now so I pull on my hood, tighten the toggles and zip up my coat to the chin. It takes some persuasion but Paddy eventually leaves his digging to head back across the field with me. On the way home I ask Paddy how much of a trim I should ask Kris to give me as lockdown haircut number two. I think the beautiful long hair of the sheep has made me reluctant to lose too much!

FEBRUARY

MONDAY 8TH FEBRUARY 2021
7:30AM : 1 DEGREE C.

Snow day! Yesterday we had snow on and off all day but, much to my disappointment, it didn't settle. However, the temperature plummeted overnight and we awoke to a nice dusting of the white stuff. Having had my eyes trained keenly on the sky whilst I ate my breakfast, I was delighted to see snowflakes begin to fall again.

Paddy is now squeaking and pacing around my legs as I put on layer upon layer in an attempt to keep the arctic chill at bay. Finally ready, I open the door and watch Paddy excitedly sniffing at this novel stuff which he has such little experience of. I follow him out and then laugh as he tries to turn too quickly and skids on the decking which is now coated white.

The first part of our walk is on the pavements and I'm taking tentative steps to test out how slippery it is. I've got Paddy closer to me and keep reminding him to "go steady" so as not to pull me like a sled dog! I can see one other pair of footprints but, aside from this, it doesn't look like many people have ventured out yet. I'm pleased when we reach the grassy footpath and feel much more confident in my chances of staying vertical!

We make our way across the first field before pausing at the fence line where Paddy always likes to do some digging in the rabbit holes. I leave him to do this important business, shaking my head at how filthy he is getting in the process- a good 70% of his usually black head is now brown. He also now appears to be wearing brown socks. I take a few photos of the white landscape while I'm waiting.

This next part of the field has been flooded in places for a couple of months, meaning wellies are essential to get through. Yesterday I noticed a tiny slit in the side of my right welly, near my big toe. Concerned that I'm about to get a very wet foot, I leap my way across, trying to ensure my right boot lands on the snow-covered lumps of ground as opposed to the icy dips. I am triumphant and, with two dry feet, we continue through the gate towards dryer land.

We've changed direction now, resulting in the bitter wind blasting snow at the side of my face. My cheek feels numb and I've got snow in my eye but I won't complain because this is the weather I've been wanting for months! We emerge onto the lane which is covered, with no sign of tyres or footprints. There's something very special about making those first prints in freshly fallen snow and I look fondly at those perfectly formed paw prints that Paddy is leaving as he trots on ahead. When I catch up, he is waiting patiently at the railway crossing for my permission to cross over. He's so good. As we continue along the lane I giggle to myself because the snow is coming down heavily now and I just love it. I pan the sky with my eyes and see that, all around, it is grey and dark with the promise of much more to come.

Further on, Paddy stops to sniff and I notice just how quiet it is. There is no traffic, no aeroplanes, no people. The only sounds I can hear are rooks 'cawing' in the trees behind us and the soft patter of snowflakes landing on my coat. Combined with the landscape around me which is now a white-out, this silence is beautiful. This moment is beautiful. How lucky am I to be stood here right now, experiencing this beauty?

As we start to head back towards the town, we encounter various people- dog walkers, individuals making their way to the shop and a few families. I smile as a small child in a bright red snowsuit rushes onto the snow-covered cricket field, unsteady on his feet. The sheer wonder on his face is a tell-tale sign that he's not experienced the joy of snow before. I hope he loves it as much as I do.

In front of the church, bright yellow crocuses were on the way out but, today, they are firmly closed like eyelids shut tight, not wanting to see the harsh conditions they are now surrounded by. The churchyard and church itself look incredibly picturesque though. In fact, I'd go so far as to say everything looks a bit more beautiful in the snow. This tree, for example, which we walk past multiple times every week, today takes on a whole new appearance which completely stops me in my tracks and I just have to capture it in a photograph. Greenery too, whether it's the evergreen firs, the spiky holly or the berries on someone's garden shrub, is all transformed by the covering of soft snow.

I may be 32 but today I feel about 7 years old, genuinely giddy at the prospect of a snow day.

MONDAY 22ND FEBRUARY 2021
7:40AM- 9 DEGREES C.

I've opted for walking boots over wellies this morning- the first time this year! The walk we're doing is mostly hard under foot with just one stodgy section which I'm hopeful I can traverse. It feels great not to be in waterproof trousers and wellies!

Not far into our walk I see a man with two spaniels in the field on the other side of the road and I can almost feel my temperature rise a few degrees. Last week I watched in disbelief as he stood watching both of his dogs poo and then walked off. I called him out on it: "I think your dogs have just been to the toilet over there" and waved my own poo bag in the air. He headed in the direction I was pointing but as soon as I'd turned around he walked off again! I didn't pursue it because I think he lives at the end of that track and I'm not 100% sure if he owns any of that land (although a lot of dog walkers use the field he allowed his dogs to poo in!) Thankfully we're not going that way today so I don't need to face him again.

As we turn down the footpath I'm pleased to see that the field ahead looks clear of livestock so I let Paddy off his lead. He's excited to get over to the rabbit holes for a good dig. I use this time to just look around me. The buds are starting to become more visible on the trees now- particularly my favourite hawthorn which is always the first to bloom a brilliant white. I can hear and see the traffic passing in the distance and am grateful that I'm not in one of those vehicles, rushing to get somewhere. Instead I'm seemingly in this opposing world where the distant traffic noise is overpowered by bird song close by. I am not rushing to get to work; I am standing still and embracing the moment. I am not stressed; I am calm.

As we walk along the lane I am on the lookout for some signs of Spring. I know it's on the way because we now have snowdrops and crocuses out in the garden and it's a lot milder. I'm hoping I might spot some celandines or perhaps the odd primrose or daffodil. A sound then interrupts my thoughts and makes me smile. It is the unmistakable bleat of a lamb, calling for its mother. I shoot my gaze through the hedge to where the call is coming from and, in the distance, spot two beautiful black lambs- one is laying down and the other is standing beside it, clearly more concerned that their mother has wandered off! I scan across and see a few more lambs, all stuck close to their mothers' sides. They've obviously only recently been turned out into the field and the lambs are still very young. This is evident from the way they are still so timid and sticking close together. Soon they will be playful and curious, exploring their surroundings and racing around in 'lamb gangs'. Oh how I love that part!

I'm brought rapidly back into the present moment by Paddy shooting off ahead. I didn't see what he was chasing but the way he is now pacing around the bottom of a tree leads me to believe it was a squirrel! I clip him back on the lead as we're now approaching a proper road anyway.

Near the cricket ground, on our way back, we meet an older lady walking on her own. I give her a wide berth (social distancing is still in place due to Covid) and say "good morning" but she stops and wants to stroke Paddy. The lady then goes on to tell me how she recently lost her dog but still goes out for the same walks as she doesn't know what else to do. I stay and talk to her for a few minutes and am left with a great appreciation for Paddy and the company he provides me with. Losing a dog is really hard. For an older person, possibly living alone, it must be unbearable. I hope the lady at least finds some comfort from her walks.

I'm delighted to see that, up ahead, there are more sheep and lambs in the field next to the pavement- much closer than those I spotted fifteen minutes ago. When we reach them we stop for a few minutes. The lambs are incredibly cute with their fluffy little faces, soft ears and uncoordinated limbs. I could watch them for hours but notice that the ewes are wary and keeping a very close eye on Paddy. I watch as a lamb skits off to her mother who stands nuzzling her head protectively.

On the way back, through the church yard, the carpet of yellow crocuses in front of the church is looking lovely. This, combined with seeing the first lambs of the year and being able to wear walking boots, has made for a very pleasant walk. I feel that the word 'pleasant' is hugely underrated. We could all do with a bit more 'pleasant' in our lives.

FRIDAY 26TH FEBRUARY 2021
7:45AM : 5 DEGREES C.

What a beautiful day! There was a frost last night and some of it remains on the car windscreens and the more shaded areas of grass. I don't think it will hang about long though as the sun is shining and there's not a cloud in the sky. Definitely another day for walking boots and, this morning, I've even swapped my big waterproof coat for a more casual one.

I've decided, as it's such a lovely day and I have nothing to rush back for this morning, that we will do a longer walk of about 90 minutes. I've not done this particular walk in about 5 months and Paddy's face lights up as we turn right instead of left at the cricket ground. The first part of the walk is along the quiet road, past the care home. We then reach a style into a field. Paddy squeezes through the gap underneath but it's rather more precarious for me traversing the style because the farmer has dug a trench round the field which has uprooted the plank I need to stand on. It's kind of like standing on a wobble board! No injuries sustained, I notice that the usual hedge line on the far side of the field has gone. It is now just two huge heaps of branches. Clearly this trench has been dug right around the perimeter. I'm sure there must be a good reason for it but it seems a shame when hedgerows provide such a haven for wildlife.

In the next field there are usually sheep but I can see they've been moved into the following one so I'm able to let Paddy off lead for a few minutes. When we do reach the sheep, I'm delighted to see them with lambs. I enjoy watching them skipping about and feeding while their mothers keep a watchful eye on Paddy and I as we make our way through. We emerge onto the quiet road again and walk past the large farm and cottage. A little further on I spot something in the fence. It's not really the right habitat around here for deer but that is my initial thought due to the size. As we get closer I can see that it is, in fact, a fox. I imagine he tried jumping the fence but got his back leg caught and then couldn't get free. It's so sad because he otherwise looks like he was incredibly healthy with a gorgeous thick, orange coat and he's big- he was clearly getting enough to eat! I hope he wasn't supporting a vixen who would be having cubs in the next few months.

We reach the track, off from the road, where Paddy can now be properly off lead. I love this part of the walk as, on the left, there is a river and, on the right, open fields. The track gradually inclines to become a ridge and from here I have a perfect 360 degree view and, as it's such a clear day, I can see for miles. Down in the river below, a family of six swans are gliding past and I notice that several of them are holding up their wings. I think they're soaking up the morning sunshine! All I can hear is my own footsteps and various birdsongs. With the sun on my face and Paddy trotting contentedly ahead I breathe in a deep lung-full of fresh countryside air and it feels wonderful.

At the bridge, we usually just cross over it but today I notice the steps leading down to a ledge. I don't know whether the steps have been cleared and are therefore more visible or, because I've not walked this way in months, I'm seeing things with fresh eyes. Anyway, I'm drawn to the steps so walk down them and then sit myself down on the ledge. I'm now sat, legs dangling over the water, looking through the bridge from below as though I'm in a tunnel. Paddy is peering over the top of the bridge at me, clearly wondering what on earth I'm doing down here! As I sit here swinging my legs, looking through the bridge and up at Paddy I consider how odd it is that, in the hundreds of times I've walked this way, I've never seen the river from this angle! Spontaneity and curiosity can be so valuable.

Further on, I notice that more gorse flowers are appearing. The lovely aroma is not here yet but the bright yellow petals certainly brighten up the footpath. I look across at the lakes and watch the birds gliding across. A couple of coots call to each other at the water's edge and a duck flaps its wings. The water is so still though, there's hardly a ripple.

Towards the end of our walk, as if on cue, the church bells chime nine times just as we're walking through the church yard. We'll be back home by 9:15am and ready for the day after this lovely start.

MARCH

SUNDAY 14TH MARCH 2021
11:30AM : 10 DEGREES C.

Paddy is very excited to see me get my big rucksack out the loft and pack it with lunch, water, his collapsible bowl, treats and poo bags. He knows this is indicative of an exciting walk! Today is Mother's Day so I've arranged to meet my Mum for a walk and picnic at Rye Harbour Nature Reserve. We're still in lockdown but meeting (and having a picnic) with one other person outside is now permitted so we're taking advantage of that. Bag packed and boots on, we jump in the car and make our way to Rye.

The car park is very busy- clearly lots of other people have had the same idea as us- but we park up okay. I put Paddy's harness on and, as I'm clipping it up, he's squeaking and shaking with anticipation and excitement. It's been months since we've walked anywhere different to our weekly walks from home! Lead on, Paddy practically drags me across the car park to reach the first patch of fresh scents and then jolts me again when he catches sight of Mum who is already here. Needless to say, he's pleased to see her- as am i!

Together we make our way along the main path which is busy with families, dogs, bikes and pushchairs. We're going to walk the long way round so soon turn off to the right and I'm able to let Paddy off lead. He's delighted at this and can't decide whether it's more important to sniff all the new smells or greet all the new dogs so he does a bit of both. Mum directs us down a bank and along the grass next to a river. I don't think I've been this way before so it's great to see where it leads. Up ahead, there is a family with a big labradoodle so I call Paddy closer to me for a treat. The labradoodle bounds over and I sense the two of them will get on well so give Pads the "okay" and they bounce around together for a while as we continue on.

As we leave the river and join a gravel path I can see how it connects with the path I've used before- it's handy that I now have this other route option. It's a lovely day- sunny skies with some cloud and a bit of a breeze- and to actually be catching up with Mum in person feels wonderful. We're chatting away happily when Mum notices some violets. We stop and admire their dark purple petals, so small and delicate but a sure sign that Spring is on the way. The buds on the trees are opening too, gradually revealing the fresh, light green leaves which are yet to unfurl.

About half way round the nature reserve we reach a crossroads and catch sight of a beautiful array of hyacinths on a grassy bank. It is the end of someone's garden and there are daffodils too but it's the hyacinths which really stand out. I'm not sure I've ever seen them in so many different colours. Along with the usual pinks and blues there are stunning purples, magenta, white, yellow and even orange. This is clearly the perfect sunny spot for them as they're already in full bloom and are dazzling. Having admired this garden, we decide to take advantage of the well-placed bench here to sit and have our lunch. After a quick drink and a bonio, Paddy eyes-up our cheese and pickle rolls, his focus so strong that he accidentally puts his foot in his water bowl. Whilst we enjoy our rolls, grapes and home-made ginger cake, we are passed by couples, families, cyclists and dogs of all shapes and sizes. I have left Paddy off lead and, for the most part, he stays right by us (he's still holding out for some of our cheese!) although a Springer Spaniel does take his fancy and he trots off to say hello. Two separate people have dogs requiring space, evident from the yellow lead and wording of one and a high-visibility jacket of the other so I hold on to Paddy whilst they pass. This is a really great initiative and, assuming people take notice and act appropriately, should make life so much easier and less stressful for those dogs-and their owners.

After lunch we continue on (much to Paddy's delight- he was becoming impatient!) and Mum cracks out her gloves. We've not been on this path long when, up ahead, near the old lifeboat station is a man and a Vizsla. The Vizsla is off lead and has laid down, watching Paddy approach, as though he's ready to pounce in a playful attack. Paddy and the Vizsla jump around a bit together before Paddy starts humping him. The man is not happy and shouts at me that his dog will bite mine if he's mounted. I rush over, apologising and pull Paddy away. This is not the first time Paddy's humping has got us in trouble and I'm certain it won't be the last. He's so good in pretty much all other areas but humping...humping is definitely his vice. I think he's now got excited as he's found a large bit of driftwood to prance around with. No longer content to play on his own, he has come over to us to proudly display his wood and encourage us to engage. Mum caves and throws the wood about five times before we tell him we've had enough. Up ahead it's getting busier with people so I put Paddy's lead back on, keen to avoid a repeat of Vizsla-humping-gate.

The building work on the fancy new visitor centre is still going on so the path narrows right down as we pass it. The view from where it stands is fantastic- it looks right over all of the wetlands- so it'll be wonderful once it's finished. We make our way back into the car park where Paddy enjoys a long drink of water and Mum and I agree how nice it was so see each other again. We're all hopeful now that this really is the beginning of the end of Covid and the associated restrictions. With tired legs but full hearts we both get back in our cars to head home.

THURSDAY 25TH MARCH 2021
7:45AM : 8 DEGREES C.

We're now officially into Spring, following the Spring equinox on Saturday and today certainly looks and feels like it. Consequently, we're now approaching that time of year when it's difficult to know what to wear on a walk. I am debating not wearing a coat but remember I need somewhere to put my phone, key, poo bags etc. so stick with the coat and fill the pockets.

Paddy and I make our way up to the cricket ground where the blossom on some of the hawthorn trees is looking beautiful now. I also spot a covering of deep purple violets amidst the grass. Paddy trots off happily ahead once I've unclipped his lead and then a flapping to my right causes me to turn. The source of this flapping is a starling looking sleek, shiny and speckled with a large twig in her beak- clearly good nesting material! She carries it away with purpose.

Further along the track we meet a couple with their Cocker Spaniel, Fin, who performs his usual routine of pulling towards me and then seemingly melting on the floor in a wiggly, waggy Spaniel greeting of fur and legs! Meanwhile, Paddy just continues on his way- he has no time for niceties, there are things to sniff! Greetings complete (on my part at least!), we go through the kissing gate and walk along past the lakes which are a beautiful bright blue with the sun shining down on them. Various different wildfowl are calling, diving, splashing and swimming and I notice two unusual looking birds with ridiculously long red bills walking on the grassy bank.

So many more plants are coming into life now. The brambles all along this footpath now have green leaves- the first sign of what's to come. In September I will be walking along here filling containers with lovely, ripe blackberries ready to fill up my freezer. In the field beyond the brambles, the rape is beginning to flower. It won't be long before it's a beautiful field of gold. Much to my delight, the gorse is flowering more profusely now too and, aided by the warmth of the sun on the flowers, when I take a deep inhale that gorgeous coconut-y scent hits me. After climbing the style and giving Pads the "okay" to come through the gap I stop to take a photo of a hawthorn tree. The fluffy white blossom looks stunning against the backdrop of the clear blue sky and flanked by the splattering of yellow in the rape field. Paddy is then very excited when I announce we're going the "long way" and races off ahead.

There are some very large holes which have been dug at the edge of the field further on. I've been watching them evolve over the past few weeks and am still unsure if they are home to foxes or badgers. I suspect foxes as badgers usually have more entry points to their sett. As we approach this area I secretly hope we might see some fox cubs. It's approaching the time of year now and we were lucky enough to see some last year, albeit in a different location. Today though there is nothing to be seen.

Paddy clambers down the river bank to get a drink before we cross the stone bridge and head along the ridge. It is so incredibly peaceful here. All that I can hear is birds chirping busily. All I can see is fields gradually turning yellow, the bright blue sky, the river glistening in the morning sunlight and some farm vehicles going about their work in the distance. A very gentle breeze brushes my face and I savour the moment of calm. As we walk along, I notice a swan at the edge of the river below. She is in the reeds and building herself a nest, pulling the reeds around herself with her beak. Spring, of course, is when most birds and animals are preparing to have their young.

The end section of the walk is all just on the road but it's a very quiet one so we're not passed by many vehicles. We pass the fields of sheep and it's lovely to see the lambs- some are busy, on their knees, feeding from their mothers; others are just basking on their sides in the warm sunshine. The grass is so green and lush! In the distance I can see a number of tractors in the field we sometimes walk across. As we get nearer I can see that they are planting potatoes. It's interesting to watch the process and how it's all running like clockwork. One small tractor lifts up a wooden crate of potatoes and tips them into the bucket of a larger tractor which then drives the length of the field, depositing them. There are two other tractors which follow behind. It looks like one may be covering the soil over the potatoes and the other adding a fertiliser. The field where they're working is alive with seagulls who are clearly enjoying the process!

eagerly for his snack too. Joo and I have both brought cheese and pickle sandwiches (great minds think alike!) which we're tucking into. We then notice some dog walkers in the distance so I hold on to Pad's lead. A few minutes later, one of the women is shouting "Hector, biscuit!" (a biscuit was never going to trump a picnic!) as her chocolate Labrador makes a beeline for us. Paddy is delighted by our new lunch companion and proceeds to hump him. I abandon my sandwich and get to my feet to haul Paddy off Hector as his owner reaches us, apologising for the interruption. Of course, we don't mind and go on to have a conversation with her about her other dog- an unusual (but beautiful) looking rescue which she's had for 13 years. The dog walkers then continue on their way and, peace restored, I sit back down to enjoy the rest of my lunch. Why is it that a packed lunch eaten mid-walk always tastes so much better?

With full tummies and Paddy beginning to whine we continue on our way. We cross more fields, walk up farm tracks and paths winding through woodland. Then we reach the most beautiful, magical place. We've climbed some steep steps to a wooded path and, on our left, our breath is taken away by a sea of blue flowers. At first, we assume they're bluebells but they're a lighter blue and much more dainty, plus it's too early for bluebells. This stunning array is behind a fence and there is a large wooden gate in the middle of the fence. The gate has a lovely, intricate black ironwork design in the middle, acting like a window to this magical fairyland. As we look through we see a path through the flowers and a large bush in bloom with pink flowers too. We admire all of this for a while and I take a few photos before we move on.

Towards the end of our walk Paddy finds a very large stick (branch!) which he proudly races through the long grass with. He's certainly enjoying today's adventure somewhere new! We re-join the footpath we started on and come out in the high street, then walk back along to the pub car park. Paddy looks pretty worn out from all the excitement and the unexpected heat so, after a drink, he hops in the boot of the car and quickly falls fast asleep whilst Joo and I continue chatting. In fact, we continue chatting for about another half an hour- clearly the two hour walk wasn't long enough for us! It was so lovely to see her again though and we couldn't have asked for a better day for it. I also thoroughly enjoyed the route which was brand new to me and it was perfect in terms of no livestock but also no styles! We didn't have to lift Paddy up once which was a refreshing change.

APRIL

THURSDAY 22ND APRIL 2021
7:45AM : 7 DEGREES C.

We've just reached the cricket ground and my gloves are off already although it is windy today so I am glad of my coat. Paddy has slowed down to a slink as we approach the sheep field because he wants to go that way but I explain to him that we'll go that way tomorrow but, today, we're going to carry on along the track to do the long walk (I like to think he understands me).

It's a beautiful day today with mainly blue sky, a few clouds and I think it's going to be warm again. As we walk along the path next to the lakes, I notice that the leaves on the brambles have fully formed now. Below the bramble bushes there are loads of nettles that have all sprung up, looking green and lush. The field just up ahead on the left is now a fantastic bright yellow. All of the rape is now in full flower which is giving this beautiful carpet of golden yellow which just looks so bright and cheery.

We've reached the gorse now which is flowering more and more. This, combined with the rape, has just made this path so bright and inviting. I take a big inhale of the gorse flowers which smell absolutely gorgeous- that real summery, coconut scent. From here we head across two fields towards Brett Aggregate where we follow the path around the side. We then reach a point where the footpath splits two ways and Paddy has, as per usual, laid down on the path he wants us to take. Luckily for Paddy, that is the way we're going today and he's delighted when I give him the "okay", rushing off ahead. Along here there are lots of dandelions, as well as some lovely clusters of red dead nettle in shades of lilac and mauve.

At the corner of the field I have a quick look at the holes which I'm still not certain belong to a fox or badger but there doesn't seem to be any new signs of activity. We continue on along the edge of this field which is now full of rape and looking lovely. At the side there are lots more nettles, along with "sticky weed" (cleavers). All the trees along here which previously had little grey fuzzy buds now have these really soft green buds with leaves coming on behind them.

We're now at the river where Paddy has gone down the bank for a drink. Over towards Camber, I can see thick black smoke billowing up. It looks too much to be a bonfire so I hope there's not a barn on fire or a car accident. I can't see any flames, just lots of this thick, black smoke. In a moment, we'll be crossing the bridge over the river to follow the path along parallel with the water. However, in the field, there is one of the farmer's big watering devices for the crops. They work by gradually turning in a circle, shooting out a huge jet of water as they go. Unfortunately, the path we need to walk is right in the firing line! We approach slowly, with me trying to judge when the jet will be pointing in the opposite direction. As we get closer I notice that there is a rainbow! It has been created by the combination of the sunshine and the spray of water and is beautiful! Paddy decides to make a run for it and veers out into the field to avoid the worst of it. I realise that, because of the wind, even when the jet is pointing the other way, the spray is still being blown across the path. There's no option but to make a run for it- so I do, screaming as I go!

Slightly damp, we carry on along the ridge with the river below and I see a swan enjoying the morning sun. It's very windy on this ridge so I'm now definitely appreciative of my coat! All of the wind turbines are spinning round in the distance and I can see lots of tractors in the fields making the most of the good weather. It really is beautiful here; there are no other people around, only Paddy and I enjoying the countryside (which is just how I like it) and all I can hear are birds happily singing. I then notice a swan in a nest at the edge of the river. She's perched up on her throne of carefully woven reeds and, right now, she's curled up with her head tucked under her wing looking very cosy. Perhaps it was her mate I saw further back.

Unfortunately we now have to walk all along the road for the final part of the walk because there are two styles where there is now no means for Paddy to get through. I can't lift him over safely on my own and don't want to risk him jumping for fear he'll hurt himself. It's incredibly frustrating when no provision is made for dogs and I think I'll get in touch with the council's footpaths team to highlight it.

The lambs are still out in the fields but they're not so small any more (still cute though!). As we turn the sharp corner I hear the unmistakable call of a peacock. Yes, a peacock. There is a manor house just here that has peacocks and they frequently roam the area.

We've had them in our garden before (much to Paddy's horror!) and they're a bit of a nuisance. Whilst I stop to try to spot the peacock, Paddy attempts to pull out a huge branch from the grass verge. I tell him it's too big and offer a smaller alternative but he's really unimpressed with this option. Eventually he begrudgingly leaves the branch and trots on.

As we walk along past the care home there are numerous rooks and jackdaws flying around and nesting in the trees. Kris and I recently did a bit of research into the corvid family of birds as we have loads of these birds around where we live and we've never been sure if they're crows, jackdaws, rooks or ravens and how to tell the difference. We now know that most of the ones we have round here are a mixture of rooks and jackdaws. Rooks are the larger of the two and have a really big, silver-grey beak. Jackdaws, however, have a very small beak, very distinctive pale eyes and a silvery sheen on the back of their head. We've noticed that the two of them seem to work together.

As we head back towards the church I notice how much all of the verges have suddenly sprung into life. There are some bluebells along here, the grass has gone wild, there's a lovely cluster of celandine, more dandelions and the cow parsley is appearing. It just looks lovely!

MAY

THURSDAY 20TH MAY 2021
7:20AM : 10 DEGREES C.

We've walked up to the cricket ground and there is a man with a lovely, young black Labrador. He has it in a "sit, stay" position and is walking in a wide circle around it, clearly working hard on the training. I watch as the dog looks around at the various distractions of other dog walkers but it stays put! It's really nice to see someone putting in the effort to train their dog properly. As we reach the car park, Paddy spots Pauline (an older lady we see regularly) who was just about to get in her car but Paddy rushes over to her, sits down and performs his best 'good boy' display. She duly rummages in her bag and gives him the usual two treats which he is very pleased with and then comes trotting back to me looking very proud of himself.

We've now reached the sheep field so I put Paddy back on his lead. There aren't actually any sheep in here today but I've got him close regardless as I know that, given the chance, he would be picnicking on all the sheep poo and, potentially, potatoes! We go through the very rickety gate on the far side which is in serious need of repair and make our way along the very narrow footpath. This path has now become very overgrown. The past couple of weeks the weather has, thankfully, got that bit warmer (the frosts have finally passed) and, this week particularly, we've had quite a bit of rain so this combination has just made everything suddenly spring into life. The grass here is near the top of my wellies; nettles have sprung up to knee height and, a little further on, there's a patch of cow parsley which is now almost shoulder height! Cow parsley just seems to grow so rapidly.

We make our way along the path which runs behind the lakes, go through the metal gate and out into the field. In the next field the farmer has now marked the footpath properly by spraying something on the crops to kill them off, just on the footpath strip. Having followed this, we now enter the rape field and this crop has shot up even more now to almost shoulder height. The flowers are still a lovely, bright yellow and I watch a fuzzy bumblebee collecting the pollen from one of the flowers. Paddy is waiting by the river for me to catch up, eating some grass in the meantime. Once I reach him we both continue together, down the edge of the rape field with the hedge on our right. This hedgerow has just exploded with life- big thistles have now appeared; different grasses, waist high; nettles; cleavers, it's all looking very lush and green.

It's nice that it's not raining today. We had a lot of very heavy rain, hail and thunder yesterday. Today seems that bit calmer- cloudy but no rain. At the end of this field we reach the area where the two big holes are and there seems to be a lot more fresh earth that has been dug out. The left hand hole doesn't seem to be in use anymore but the right hand one has definitely had some recent activity. The red dead nettle around the corner is looking very nice and there are some buttercups out as well. As I walk along this slightly precarious path (it's very narrow and sloped!), Paddy looks back at me from up ahead to see where I've got to (clearly we don't have time to dilly-dally looking down holes- I'll remember that, Pads!). I can hear lovely birdsong as birds chirp away in the bushes beside me and we make our way around the edge of Brett Aggregate. In the next field we're approaching I can see the sheep are near the gate so attach Paddy's lead. As we walk around the sheep I think about how good Paddy is and the progress he's made. He's walking so calmly next to me, not batting an eyelid at the sheep. Obviously I'd never risk having him off lead around sheep but I appreciate how good he is.

We walk along the front side of the lakes now and the gorse here has died back a bit but the hawthorn is looking beautiful with its dainty little white flowers and shiny green leaves. I also notice that, in the river, some of the first water irises are coming out- bold yellow flowers. We continue along the path, back towards the cricket ground.

In the churchyard, I can't help but feel a little disappointed by the cherry tree this year. Normally, this tree is just absolutely breath-taking, laden with lovely white/pink blooms. This year, however, it's just not as good. I don't know whether it's because we've not had as many of those really sunny days with a bright blue sky to provide a backdrop for it to stand out or if it's just not performed as well for some reason. I continue to ponder this as we head back home.

THURSDAY 27TH MAY 2021
7:10AM- 13 DEGREES C.

I'm not sure what to wear this morning for our walk because it's warm (and will be getting warmer), sunny and there is not much cloud so I don't really need a coat but neither my trousers or jumper have sufficient/secure enough pockets for my phone, key, poo bags etc. I always have this dilemma around this time of the year! In the end I opt for a lighter coat (for the pockets) and no jumper.

We make our way past all the usual houses and church and on up the road towards the cricket ground. As I look around up here I appreciate what a lovely day it is. After a very wet, cold May it's really nice to have a bit of sunshine again and feel the warmth- like it should be at this time of the year. The grass in the sheep field has got quite long, due to the recent absence of sheep in here presumably, so my boots are getting quite wet. I opted for walking boots as I knew I'd get too hot in wellies but the boots (and bottoms of my trousers) are getting soaked!

The path after the rickety gate is now massively overgrown. Where the trees are now adorned with leaves and blossom, they're really hanging over the path so it's a case of tip-toeing along, hanging on to and leaning over the fence to avoid being taken out by the foliage. One downside to the warmer weather , which I'm noticing along this path, is that all the midges come out. They are currently all flying around my face which is not very pleasant! As I attempt to bat away the midges I round the corner where the nettles are now way above my knees, as are the cleavers. It won't be long now before I'm forced to find a large stick to beat the nettles back a bit to create a clear passageway through.

Paddy bounds off ahead, seemingly not bothered by the overgrown path, whilst I stop to admire the lakes. They are looking beautiful, just glistening in the early morning sunshine and there is very little wind today so the water is calm and peaceful. Once I've caught up with Paddy, I open the gate for us to continue on across the fields. The crops on either side here have started to grow quite significantly. I think it is corn as it looks like there are some ears of corn beginning to appear. I'll watch how it progresses over the coming weeks.

In the rape field I stop to remove my coat and instantly feel much more comfortable as I tie it around my waist and enjoy the very slight breeze on my bare arms. Walking through here I notice that the rape has definitely passed its peak. There are a number of flowers that have died off now so it doesn't look as vivid yellow as before but more 'speckled' as I look across the field.

For the past few weeks I've not been well. I've been going through rather a lot but it's really nice to be out in the countryside, walking Paddy and not seeing anyone. I find it very healing just having this space, quiet and solitude to think things through whilst being immersed in nature. Looking about and noticing plants, insects and birds just helps. It makes you realise that nature doesn't stop; things come and go; seasons change; the day closes and another sunrise comes in the morning- all very comforting reminders that I think are worth keeping in mind. Nothing lasts forever. I consider how, with crops, farmers have good years and bad. Sometimes things don't grow properly or perform as well but the following year everything falls into place with the weather, conditions etc. and they harvest a bumper crop.

At the riverbank I look across at the wind turbines which, today, are all completely still as there is insufficient wind to drive them. Paddy goes down the bank to have a paddle and drink. As he does so I notice there are a number of aquatic plants all visible and growing well, along with a nice clump of water irises.

We emerge from the end of the path at the corner of Brett Aggregate and Paddy catches the scent of something and sprints off ahead, down the side of the field. I turn the corner and catch a glimpse of him very close to the point where I know the fence is low. I run down the field after him but then he is gone. I reach the fence which is all battered and bent over and know that Pads has jumped it (it's really no height at all). There is no sign of him at all so I stand here calling and whistling. Nothing. After about five minutes I decide to step over the fence and walk up to stand on top of a mound. From here I can see that what I was hoping was a river (and thus being a barrier for him) actually has no water in so he could easily have gone straight across it. I scan around, a sinking feeling in my stomach, as I realise this means he could potentially now be in a field of sheep on the other side, possibly get out onto the main 60mph road, and could definitely be in the quarry where there are diggers, machinery and goodness knows what other dangers! I continue calling and whistling but there are still no signs of him. I'm now really starting to panic as it's been a good ten minutes he's been gone and I'm starting to question what I'm actually going to do. At what point should I phone Kris? Then, just as I'm running through all the scenarios in my mind, I hear something and see the reeds moving in the distance. I call Paddy enthusiastically and am relieved to see the movement in the reeds coming closer towards me. He emerges from the reeds absolutely exhausted, tongue hanging out and looking in the river bed for some water to drink. Once he is back up on my side of the bank I quickly clip his lead back on. As frustrated as I am at his escapades, I'm flooded with relief to have him back and for him being okay. He will be staying on the lead for the remainder of the walk now!

Considering there is a very dangerous quarry there, I think it's pretty poor that the fencing is so derelict. I appreciate that Paddy shouldn't have gone off chasing something but if the fencing was more secure and properly maintained he wouldn't have been able to get through there. I think I'll have to look into who to contact to report it and ask if it can be repaired.

I find somewhere for Paddy to have a good drink and then we make our way home…very slowly as he has well and truly exhausted himself!

JUNE

TUESDAY 8TH JUNE 2021
7:10AM : 15 DEGREES C.

This morning we are making our way past the play park and out into the field. Despite being warm, it is misty which feels odd. The sun is already starting to burn through the mist though and I can feel its warmth kissing my skin. There is promise of another lovely day- in fact, the whole week- but, then again, this is what the weather should be like in June. As a result of the mist, the grass is very wet this morning but thankfully I'm prepared in my wellies.

We were away last week and it's amazing just how much growth has occurred in that short space of time. You really notice it when you've been away and then come back. Out here now the corn is well above knee height and getting on for waist height. It's looking really nice but it is at this time of the year that I have to hope Paddy doesn't get the scent of something and go off into the corn field as you just can't see him at all. If you're lucky you can see the corn moving but that's about it. Thankfully this morning, so far, he is sticking to the path. I did have a quick scan around when we first entered the field because recently out here there has sometimes been a lady with two Collies. She keeps them both on an incredibly short lead and I don't know if the dogs aren't friendly or if she's just very strict and overprotective but, whenever she sees us, she walks off into the middle of the corn field. It's very sad as you can hear her shouting "leave it!" at the dogs and yanking on their short leads. I'm sure the dogs are simply interested in who we are and may like to come and say hello but there we go.

We're now walking along the edge of the second field and it's lovely to see some poppies- they're something that has appeared whilst we've been away. They are dotted along the verge here next to the river with lots of different grasses too. There are some other things growing up as well which might be rose bay willow herb but I'm not sure yet. I'll have to wait and see how they develop over the coming weeks.

Paddy is waiting patiently for me in order that we can cross the railway line together. The grass and cow parsley after the style here are very tall now (waist height) and, because of the mist and dew this morning, my legs are now soaked! Hopefully I should dry off quite quickly though as it's warm and I'm wearing my new walking trousers which are really lightweight. The other benefit of these new walking trousers is that they actually have pockets! This means I can fit my phone in, meaning I no longer have to wear a coat unnecessarily so, this morning, I've just got a jumper on and am much more comfortable as a result.

The other thing with all this mist and dew is that you can see all the cobwebs. It's strange to think that all of these cobwebs must be here every day but we just can't see them. With all the dew on them, like tiny little beads, they look almost like strings of pearls- really intricate. They're everywhere, between all of the plants.

Out in the next field where the grass is equally long I continue to get wet legs as we head towards the big wooden bridge to cross the river. Recently, I've been getting Paddy to wait at the first end of this bridge. I used to get him to wait at the other end of it but he started bolting into the next field (where the back of the runway for the airport is) due to there being lots of rabbits- and occasionally foxes- out there. I let Paddy off the lead again once we're in the field and I'm confident there are no animals around for him to race off after. He's now quite content just snacking on rabbit poo. Out here the footpath officially runs right next to the hedge but all along there are numerous rabbit holes, some of which are incredibly deep. I've walked along there so many times that I mostly know where those holes are and can dodge them but where the grass has now grown so much it has covered them so it's impossible to see where they are, making it dangerous to navigate. I've come a cropper a few times along there, losing my leg up to the knee down a hole! Consequently, this morning, I'm using a path that runs parallel to it, a bit further into the field which is, thankfully, free of holes.

We're heading to the end of this field and there are lots of buttercups out here. At the end there is all of the gorse, though it's no longer in flower. It's quite an unusual environment just here. There are lots of pebbles under foot as a result of being so close to the coast; there is all the gorse; teasels that come up through the pebbles; and plants that look like mint but, upon rubbing the leaves, it doesn't smell like it. Perhaps it's from the same family though. Over the fence there are numerous bramble bushes which will be laden with blackberries later in the year. I often pick some from here. Paddy is currently gorging himself on rabbit poo so I'm going to move him along and we'll start heading back.

I've just heard a cuckoo-that really distinctive "coo koo" which is nice to hear. The hawthorn is still looking beautiful. I can see two trees just over the river- one baring pink flowers and the other white, looking very pretty. I also notice some purple vetch at my feet just starting to come out which is a nice wildflower. I'm on the bridge now and Paddy is in the water below, having a refreshing drink. As I look down I notice how tall all of those aquatic plants have become. What used to just be a clear river is now covered with all of these aquatic plants and there is a beautiful flower amongst them. It has a very tall stem and lovely pink petals with more buds ready to open.

We've now crossed back over the railway and I'm stood on the style which acts as a good vantage point to scan across the fields. I see no sign of the lady with the Collies which is good. Normally, if I see her, I put Paddy on his lead as I obviously don't want him bombing over to say hello and upsetting her further. The sun is really burning off the mist now, revealing the church in the distance and patches of blue sky above. It won't be long now before a clear summer's day emerges.

SATURDAY 26TH JUNE 2021
8:30AM : 16 DEGREES C.

We're heading up towards the cricket ground and I'm already feeling warm, despite just being in a t-shirt. There are a few people at the cricket ground as we pass but it's generally quiet. The footpath ahead which passes the lakes looks like it may have been mown and I've noticed a number of verges around the area have been cut so I really hope that means all of the footpaths are going to be cut back soon as there are a few now which have become almost impassable which is a real shame.

There are lots of fishermen at the lakes, clearly making the most of this June summer morning with bright blue skies and sunshine. We come out into the sheep field (where there are currently no sheep) and the grass here is quite long, resulting in my boots getting a bit wet. They will dry off quickly in today's heat though. Through the gate and into the next field, I can't fail to notice the huge carpet of blue out here. I have no idea if it is a crop or a wildflower but it looks absolutely beautiful. I stop to take a photo, including a close up of the flower head so I can try to identify it when I get home.

Paddy is up ahead and is ominously looking into the corner of Brett Aggregates where he previously got in and went AWOL. A pheasant now flies up, making a racket and flapping which causes much excitement for Paddy but thankfully he settles back down and continues on the path as the pheasant flies away. I catch up with Paddy and we continue around the field together, me still admiring those blue flowers. There are lots of butterflies and bumblebees enjoying the flowers too.

At the footpath junction I expect Paddy to want to take the longer route to the right but he automatically goes left- he must know it's Saturday! (this is our usual Saturday route). There is slightly more shade as we turn the corner and this proves a welcome reprieve for both Paddy and me. In the field on our right there is corn which seems to be growing up nicely and to the left is the big bank which separates us from Brett Aggregates. I can hear lots of machinery working away in there. Down the final side, Paddy keeps catching the scent of things and spotting rabbits in the distance so I have to keep reminding him to "stay on the path" and, when he gets too far ahead of me, asking him to "wait". Thankfully, he's got a very good 'wait' and I can generally get him to stop and wait from quite a distance away, allowing me to catch up with him, so that's really handy.

As we come out at the entrance to Brett Aggregates, it looks like the footpath hasn't been cut back and is massively overgrown. There is grass solidly down this footpath, all of which is almost shoulder height so we won't be going down there! Instead, we'll have to walk down the main drive for Brett Aggregates. There are signs saying "no dog walkers" but, with the footpath being impassable, I don't know what else they expect people to do. Paddy is on lead so I don't see we're doing any harm. Hopefully they'll get that path cleared soon.

We've now reached the path at the caravan park and there is a sign here which makes me laugh every time I see it. The sign is advertising having a caravan at this location and, in large writing, says "Do you want the quiet life!" This irritates me first of all because they have used an exclamation mark where it should be a question mark but the funny aspect is the irony. It couldn't be any further from the "quiet life" where this caravan park is situated. For starters, it is right on a 60mph, national speed limit road. Secondly, it's next to the army firing range and, thirdly, literally in the middle of the caravan park is a huge electricity pylon which buzzes in the rain. It just tickles me every time we walk past.

We're now continuing along the path which winds its way back into the town. There are lots of wildflowers along here at the moment including poppies, foxgloves and these lovely bluey/pinky flowers which are ubiquitous across the Marsh. I need to look them up and find out the name; they are almost thistle-like. It's very warm today. Thankfully there was a stream further back where Paddy could get a drink but I definitely don't want to be out much longer with him this morning.

I have seen lots of dragonflies today; mostly the thin, electric blue ones that dart about but I have also seen a couple of the really big ones that almost sound like mini helicopters. The part of the footpath we're on now is, thankfully, lovely and shady. Paddy and I are both very much appreciating it. We are taking our time here-

Paddy sniffing and me noting the flowers. I can see the beginnings of the rose bay willow herb and have just spotted some 'Granny pop out of bed'! I have no idea what the actual name is for them but they are big white flowers. I remember, when I was a young girl, my Mum showing me that if you squeeze the base of the flower it pops out (hence, 'Granny pop out of bed'!). I used to enjoy this small delight as a child. The honeysuckle along here with its lovely pink flowers tumbling down the fence smells divine. I take a deep inhale of this scent before we leave the footpath and make our way through the high street and back home.

WEDNESDAY 30TH JUNE 2021
7:10AM- 15 DEGREES C.

It's very cloudy today; not raining but very dull and it just doesn't feel like summer. We're into July tomorrow so I'd expect it to be a bit more hot and sunny. Anyway, at least it's not raining. We got soaked yesterday so I'll take today's dullness and cloud as an improvement! We're heading past the church and up towards the cricket ground where I deposit Paddy's poo bag in the bin and then, much to Paddy's delight, turn and tell him we're continuing up the road to do the long walk. We follow the road round, past the care home, and reach the sharp corner where the footpath goes across the field. The farmer has been doing a lot of work in this field and had blocked the small hole that Paddy used to go through whilst I climbed the style. I'm pleased to see that the barrier has now been removed though, meaning Pads can squeeze through as usual.

A crop of potatoes has been planted out here but, thankfully, the farmer has made a nice clear path straight across the field for us to follow. Paddy is excitedly trotting off ahead but, not wanting him to get to far away, I recall him and he comes bombing full pelt towards me and I have to sidestep to avoid him running straight into me! At the end of this field a lot of work has been done and the hedgerow removed (which seems a huge loss to me in terms of wildlife but I optimistically hope the farmer had good reason for this) so I hope we can still get through, which we can.

I pop Paddy on his lead as there are sheep in the next two fields. In the second of these fields I hear some "moo"ing which puts me on edge. Looking around, I spot some dairy cows up near the farm buildings and it looks like they have access to this field we're currently walking in. However, thankfully they all seem to be going in for milking or feeding. It's unusual though as there have never been cows out here before. I'll have to keep an eye on them. Thankfully it will be fairly easy to spot if they're out here from quite some distance away so I could take an alternative route to avoid them if necessary which is reassuring.

We make our way up the lane to reach the next footpath and there is a lady just coming out with her dog. We've met her once before. Her dog is quite a nervous rescue so she's not yet let her off lead. We exchange pleasantries and then Pads and I continue on and I let him off his lead. It's been a very long time since I've walked this way. The last couple of times I have, I walked it the opposite way round (the route that is, not walking backwards!) It's funny how different things look when you do a walk the opposite way to usual. You just get a completely different perspective on things. I can see things have changed since I last came along here- everything is now overgrown. Along the middle of the path is what I think is plantain which is an edible plant. I've made pesto with it before and you can treat it a bit like spinach. There's loads of it here and I'm 90% sure it's plantain but I won't pick any yet as obviously, with foraging, it's important to be 100% sure you've identified the plant correctly. When I get home I'll have a look in my foraging book to confirm it. There are two different sorts along here, although perhaps one is just the younger, fresh growth and the other is older. Also along here is both red and white clover. I think that's edible too but can't remember if it's the leaves or flower or both so that's another one for me to check!

Paddy is now waiting for me at the bridge. The water here has lots of green algae in so I won't be encouraging Pads to have a drink. We make our way down the field and, next to the hedgerow, it's got really overgrown. Following the rain we've had these past few days, my legs are getting soaked! There are big thistles along here too which I'm trying to dodge so it's not the most pleasant part of the walk but thankfully this part is not too long. At the end of this section we're rewarded with the view of the carpet of beautiful blue flowers which I first noticed at the weekend. I looked them up and it turns out it's linseed. I have milled linseed for my breakfast each morning with my oats but I had no idea what the crop looked like. It's beautiful though and it would be rather nice to see more of it around.

We will now make our way past the lakes and cricket ground to head back home for me to start work.

Plantain pesto

Ingredients:

- 80g fresh plantain
- 150ml extra virgin olive oil
- 2 garlic cloves
- 50g walnuts
- 50g hard cheese, grated

Method:

1. Rinse the foraged plantain and pat dry.
2. Add all of the ingredients to a food processor and blend until smooth.

Tips and variations:

- Keep in the fridge and use within 5 days.
- Freeze and use within 3 months.
- Any greens could be used in place of plantain- forage some wild garlic or use basil.
- Pine nuts, cashews or sunflower seeds could be used in place of walnuts.

JULY

MONDAY 19TH JULY 2021
7:20AM : 18 DEGREES C.

It's been very hot the past few days so I'd put shorts on when I woke up this morning. However, I decided to swap to my walking trousers given how overgrown it is everywhere (they've still not cut any of the footpaths back yet). I was planning on doing the cow walk today but when we reach the junction, Paddy wants to do the airport walk instead so that's the way we head.

The first few fields have corn in which must be almost ready to harvest I think. It's all dried out a lot. I hadn't anticipated it being wet underfoot but there seems to be dew from last night and the grass is soaked so I'm getting rather wet boots and trouser legs. It's so hot today that it's actually quite refreshing having wet legs though! It's such a beautiful day: bright blue sky and it's going to be another scorcher I think. It's the middle of July so really this is the weather we should expect. Thankfully it's early enough at the moment that the heat is not unbearable and there's a little bit of a breeze. I put my hands in the air and spin around 360 degrees, revelling in the fact that Paddy and I are the only ones out here. There's no sign of anyone else for miles; we're just surrounded by corn fields with the church in the distance and it's just so peaceful. I've seen a few dragonflies this morning too- some of the big helicopter ones and some of the small, electric-blue ones.

At the railway crossing it's still incredibly overgrown. This is one of the places I'd reported to the council but they've obviously not been able to get anyone out yet. We pick our way through and out into the final corn field which is equally overgrown. Over the past few weeks I've been using my feet to try to push down the corn on the footpath but it's all still waist height and you can barely see the path. In addition, it's the kind of day today where I worry there could be snakes basking on the hot ground. Consequently, we walk through very briskly and I try not to think about what might be underfoot. I'm thankful I've at least got my sturdy walking boots on.

At the bridge I put Paddy's lead on ready to cross the airport field. A couple of weeks ago we had almost reached the end of this field when Pads darted off like he often does due to there invariably being rabbits at the end on the scrubland area. However, as he reached that area there was all this screeching, snarling and hissing. At the same time I realised they were not rabbits. They were a group of animals that were a very dark colour, almost black. My mind raced to catch up with the fact they definitely weren't rabbits but couldn't place what they were. I rushed over and some of the animals had scarpered off into the gorse but one remained, very much standing its ground! I shouted at Pads to "leave it!" and he then stood there not knowing what to do. I then had to pretty much step around this animal whilst it was snarling and showing its teeth to reach Paddy and put him safely on his lead. At this point the remaining animal then scurried off into the gorse. At the time I wasn't certain what they were but I thought they might be polecats. They were definitely a weasel-y type creature, much too big to be a stoat and it was their very dark colour that made me suspect polecat. When we returned home I looked it up and discovered they definitely were polecats. It turns out, in the past, they became almost extinct and are quite rare but they're starting to make a comeback in various parts of the UK, including Southern England. It's certainly a fantastic spot for them there as it's so quiet (I think I'm probably one of the only people that regularly uses that footpath) and there are all those rabbits providing a plentiful food source for them. I was so elated and felt incredibly honoured to have seen a whole family of polecats though! Today, I have Pads firmly on lead in case they're there again but there are no signs of them.

As we head back across the field I notice some beautiful butterflies. They are white with black spots, like Dalmatians. I will try to remember to find out what they are when we return home. Paddy heads down to the river to refresh himself in the cool water and then proceeds to roll around in the grass on the bank in an attempt to dry himself off. We quickly make our way through the overgrown corn, again, trying to keep snakes free from my thoughts and cross the railway. In the next field, Paddy shoots off and several pheasants fly up out of the corn- much to Pad's delight. Job done, he now trots along the path looking very pleased with himself.

Recently I've been quite stressed about work and find myself thinking about it when I shouldn't be. I never used to be like this but with the Pandemic and a big restructure at work I've been finding it harder to switch off. It annoys me when I realise I'm thinking about work in my own time but one thing I sometimes do on my walks which always helps bring me back into the present moment is listing five things I can see, four things I can hear, three things I can feel, two things I can smell and one thing I can taste (the taste is always a tricky one).

So, five things I can see at the moment:

1. *A butterfly flitting about above the corn.*

2. *The church in the distance, standing out above all the houses.*

3. *All of the ears of corn which are a sandy colour and really dry.*

4. *A big dragonfly darting about.*

5. *Some poppies- the really thin ones that just look like tissue paper- so small and red.*

Now four things I can hear:

1. *Some birds tweeting in the hedgerow.*

2. *The swishing of my walking trousers.*

3. *Some very distant traffic around the airport.*

4. *The reeds and grasses gently blowing in the breeze.*

Three things I can feel:

1. *The soft, feather-like grasses as I brush past them.*

2. *The hard ground under my feet, solid after all of this hot, dry weather.*

3. *An ear of corn- really prickly.*

Two things I can smell:

1. *My sun cream.*

2. The grasses. We had a heavy dew last night and now the sun is burning it off, leaving behind a fresh grassy scent.

One thing I can taste:

1. I nearly always end up saying toothpaste, having always brushed my teeth just before coming out.

This activity is such a good one for focusing the mind on the here and now rather than it wandering off.

I just saw some more flying insects. I'm not sure if they were dragonflies but they were a red colour. This reminds me of a beautiful moth/butterfly I saw here last week. It was black with bright red spots and I took a lovely photo of it on some viper's bugloss (the purple flowering thistle plant). As we make our way across the final field, the church appearing closer, it is definitely getting warmer. Paddy certainly won't be getting a lunchtime walk today. In fact, I doubt I'll be able to walk him again until about 7:30pm due to this heat. Thankfully he's very flexible and adaptable and, to be honest, when it's as hot as this he's not too fussed about going out anyway- he'd far rather just lay on the hard wooden floor of our front room with the doors open so a light breeze can flow over him. Right now though, he is eyeing up a rook on the path ahead. Luckily the rook flies off so Pads doesn't have to expend any energy fending it off. Together, we now slowly make our way back home.

THURSDAY 29TH JULY 2021
7:30AM : 17 DEGREES C.

Having passed the cemetery, we now head out into the corn field. It's a nice sunny morning, although there are some black clouds around so I've got my thin jacket with me in case of a downpour. I'm also wearing my wellies because our garden looked wet and I know this walk is still very overgrown in a couple of places so I anticipated I'd probably end up getting wet. However, at the moment, it seems dry. The corn has really dried out and I've noticed some of the fields around the area have started to be cut and harvested so hopefully it won't be long until they're all cut. There is a nice breeze today. Yesterday was very windy so I'm pleased it has eased to something more pleasant and refreshing today.

Paddy is trotting ahead of me on the path, his coat glistening in the sunshine. When it's sunny like this, his black fur appears to turn an iridescent purple colour which looks beautiful. We continue up the second field with the stream on our left. There are some bulrushes emerging from the water, rose bay willow herb now with all its little pink flowers appearing, lots of tall grasses and tall yellow flowers which I need to identify. They look a little like dandelion flower heads but are much taller and more spindly. Regardless, they brighten it up nicely along here. There is also the odd poppy here and there but, by and large, they're finished now. Up ahead is the water tower which we're walking towards and, to the right, I can see Dungeness Power Station. There is some very distant traffic noise but, aside from that, it's just the rhythmic swishing of my feet brushing through the grass, little bumblebees buzzing around and the breeze gently blowing all of the grasses- a beautiful mix of relaxing sounds.

Up ahead, Paddy is on the path but peering into the corn field with pricked ears so I remind him to "stay on the path" as I really don't want him going bounding all through the corn. Thankfully he acquiesces and trots on ahead before waiting on the small wooden bridge for me to catch up. He's such a good dog. He knows he has to wait at this point for me to give him the "Okay" to carry on into the next field. It does just melt my heart a little that he's such a good boy. Along the side of this next field, where it's sheltered by trees, it's really claggy underfoot so my wellies are becoming caked in mud and getting heavier and heavier as I go (I feel like I'm walking in moon boots!) so this is a good reason for wearing the wellies.

After crossing the railway we enter the next field and Paddy gets the scent of something and dives into the corn, thankfully not too far from the path. He's pouncing around in there and I'm worried there's a snake in there that he's heard so I call him back on the path. Now a pheasant springs up out of the corn right next to me, flapping its wings madly, scaring the life out of me in the process! This is clearly what Paddy had got the scent of and I'm relieved that it's a pheasant and not a snake. Moving on, Pads goes in the river for a splash around before we cross the bridge. Once he's out I clip his lead on to head out into the airport field. Heading across here I can't see any rabbits and am hopeful that might mean the polecat family are there again. Alas, when we reach that area, there is no sign of them. I do hope I get to see them again one day as they were so unusual. There are lots of teasels that have all shot up around here in the pebbles. Whilst I'm admiring these, Paddy is shovelling in his mouth as much rabbit poo as he can before I interrupt him and we make our way back. There are so many butterflies out here now- they seem to be very much enjoying the purple flowers of the viper's bugloss. I also notice that lots of blackberries are forming amidst the brambles and some of them are even turning pink and plumping up nicely. I therefore don't think it'll be too long before we can start picking some which will be very nice so I'll have to start coming on our walks armed with Tupperware containers. As we head back home I think about the blackberry and apple crumbles and jams to be made and enjoyed later this year.

Apple & Blackberry jam

Ingredients:

- 1.8kg apples
- 900g blackberries
- ½ pint water
- 1.3kg granulated sugar
- Approx. 6 jam jars

Method:

1. Grease the bottom of the preserving pan with a bit of margarine so the jam doesn't stick.

2. Peel, core and thinly slice the apples (weighed once peeled and cored) then put in preserving pan. Add ¼ pint of water and turn on the heat to stew the apple, stirring throughout.

3. In another pan (separate pans for apple and blackberries due to different cooking times), put the washed blackberries and ¼ pint of water and stew. Whilst they're stewing, put a saucer in the fridge to cool ready for testing jam.

4. Whilst the fruits are still stewing, put the jam jars (without lids) in the oven on the lowest temperature to warm up.

5. Once both fruits are stewed, combine them and add the sugar. Stir well until the sugar has all dissolved.

6. Boil rapidly (on full heat) until setting point is reached.

7. When the jam is doing a 'rolling boil' (bubbling all over), time for 10 minutes, stirring occasionally.

8. After the 10 minutes, take a spoon full of jam out and put it on the saucer from the fridge.

Return the saucer to the fridge for 3 minutes. If the jam has set properly it should wrinkle down or be solid when the saucer is tipped up. Spoon this jam back into the pan and remove any 'scum' from the top of the jam.

9. *Remove the jars from the oven and carefully pour in the jam up to the necks of the jars.*

10. *Put waxed discs onto the top of the jam in all jars, then leave until cold before putting the lids on the jars.*

AUGUST

WEDNESDAY 4TH AUGUST 2021
7:10AM : 15 DEGREES C.

The temperature dropped to about 12 degrees last night so I've got a jumper on this morning. It's a lovely day today though- bright blue sky, some clouds but just really pleasant. I actually prefer it when it's a bit cooler but nice and bright so today is perfect as far as I'm concerned. This morning we're heading out towards the cow field. As we walk down the track and across the railway I notice that the first blackberries are ready so I go over to the bush and pick one off for myself and one for Paddy. We both chew away contentedly and it's not lost on me that there are more blackberries right next to an apple tree on the opposite side of this track. A match made in heaven! Apples and blackberries side by side, just waiting to be picked and turned into a tasty dessert.

We cross the road and take the footpath down between a few houses. I can see that the path down here has been cut back so it's much easier walking once more. I'm hopeful this means they might have also cut back the other section further on which I'd reported as being hugely overgrown. I turn the corner, cross the little bridge over the stream and see that Paddy is waiting patiently for me at the gate. I clip his lead on just in case there are any cows out here, though I can't see any at the moment thankfully. Whenever we walk this way I'm constantly scanning around to check for cows. I can now just see the silhouettes of them on the horizon, right at the other end of the field so it's good to know they're a long way away.

As we approach the overgrown section I can see, unfortunately, it hasn't been seen to yet which is very frustrating. They've done the part that really wasn't that bad and then, a couple of hundred meters on, they've not tackled this. I can only hope they're going to come back and do it another day. As I stand here tutting, Paddy yelps and rushes towards me and I hear the clicking of the electric fence so I assume he must have sniffed it or brushed his tail against it and he's been shocked. I give him some strokes to comfort him but he continues to whine so I decide to get us on the move and open the gate. Pads rushes through, clearly keen to get away from the scary fence that hurt him! I can't make it through as quickly due to the extent of growth. There are thick brambles right across the path which I try to carefully pick between my fingers and move to the side but there is another one jabbing in my neck, whilst yet another snags in my trousers. It's really awkward and unpleasant but, unfortunately, there is just no alternative route. The only other option would be to remain in the cow field but then we would have to get past the electric fence further round. I've made it through the bramble section and then have to almost crawl due to the tree branches that now span the path. The only saving grace is that this is a relatively short section of the walk and I'm now back out onto an acceptable path where I join Paddy.

Paddy has now spotted something and has gone bombing off into the corn field. I can just about see him, every now and then, leaping out the top, ears flapping up before he disappears again. Thankfully he is just at the edge, not far from the path so I continue on and allow him his few minutes of fun. When he catches up with me he is panting heavily and looking for a drink, having knackered himself out. He disappears down the bank on our way up the field towards the farm and I can hear him splashing about. When he emerges, he shakes and then rolls around in the grass to try to dry off. It can't have been fresh water but at least his body will now feel cooler, even if he does now stink...

Having crossed the railway again we continue along the lane. It's wonderfully shaded along here under the large trees and hedgerow which makes for very pleasant walking. We're flanked on either side by lots of rose bay willow herb which looks lovely with its pretty pink flowers. It's so peaceful along here- we very rarely see anyone and, despite it being a road, it's quiet enough for Paddy to be off lead. I look around at the surrounding farmland and notice the farmer doing his morning rounds feeding his sheep. Paddy keeps stopping to eat grass so I gently nudge him on before he makes himself sick. I love this part of the day though. It's probably my favourite time, where I can just be outside in the countryside where it's so still and peaceful. Standing here now, all I can hear is pigeons cooing, bumblebees buzzing around and birds tweeting in the hedgerows. It's perfect and I always feel it just sets me up so well for the day ahead just to have this calm space before I have to start work, talk to people and things start getting stressful. Yes, this is a good start and just what I need. It's almost like the countryside is my daily medication!

TUESDAY 24TH AUGUST 2021
9:30AM : 18 DEGREES C.

It's Kris' birthday today which is why we're so much later coming out this morning. It's a lovely day though- really warm and sunny and quite a bit of a breeze which is actually very nice. We're doing the airport walk this morning and, much to my delight, the corn has been cut! This has subsequently revealed many objects which have evidently been lost amongst the corn all these months. Paddy darts off to the right to claim a tennis ball (not ours but he's claiming it nonetheless!) which he is delighted with. He rushes to me with his new prize and drops it at my feet. I obligingly throw it up the path for him and wonder how long he'll carry it for. To be honest, it wouldn't surprise me if he carried it the whole way and took it home. He's pretty dedicated like that.

We're now crossing over the small wooden bridge which takes us into the next field. Right by this bridge there are some lovely wild flowers which I think are red campion and then further into this field (which, incidentally, hasn't been cut) there are some flowers which look similar to ox eye daisies but are smaller clusters on tall stems. Accompanying these are the tall, yellow dandelion-like flowers which I'm still yet to identify. It looks gorgeous out here today. I did wonder, being later than usual, if we might meet someone else out here but, so far, there is no sign of anyone else. Looking around me, all I can see is fields of corn, wild flowers, Paddy on the path up ahead, a butterfly flitting around in front of me and seagulls overhead making a bit of a racket.

I can't see Paddy now so call his name and his head has popped up from amongst the corn, just at the side of the path. I continue on the path and he disappears again. This time when I call him I get no response. Just as I'm starting to worry, I notice a patch of flattened corn and Paddy is laying there with his crazy (excited) eyes. The closer I get, the more excited he becomes until he can't contain it anymore, grabs his ball and charges off. He does make me laugh. Literally every day he makes me smile and laugh and I'm so grateful for that.

There are some poppies still hanging on out here and a beautiful little dragonfly. He's got a red body and has just landed on the corn so I'm able to get a closer look. His red body is furry, like a bumblebee. He has beautiful, transparent wings and, on his head, these big eyes scanning side to side. I let out an involuntary shocked noise as he suddenly flies straight up, like a helicopter, into my face which was peering over him. I leave him to his important business and continue on my way. All the reeds along here by the river are really blowing in this wind this morning. It makes a lovely sound though and just watching them sashaying to and fro is really relaxing. I can now see the next field we're going in to and that hasn't been cut either. They've obviously just started with the first field but hopefully the rest will be done soon too.

Paddy really is so good. We've been on annual leave this week and have has lots of days out where he's come with us and he's been great. It's so nice to have a dog we can just take out and about easily with us. He's now gone charging off up the side of the field after a rabbit. I think he's still got that ball in his mouth though...

The sun is really beating down out here. I would have worn shorts today but, with the overgrown fields, felt my walking trousers would be the more sensible option. There are more lovely butterflies along here and I really need to get better at identifying them. There is one here that has got orange and white stripes which I think might be a red admiral. I'll check when we get back home. As I turn around I see Paddy is waiting at the style for me, clearly wondering what I'm looking at which is causing the delay. I notice he's left the ball on the path here near the style- I expect his intention is to collect it from here on the way back. We cross the railway and then, as we enter the next field, a plane comes right in front of us and lands on the runway. Pads then goes down into the river for a splash about to cool off. This is followed by his usual rolling in the grass to dry off. However, today this procedure is performed on the bank as opposed to the top of the bank. Consequently, he ends up rolling back down the bank, much to my amusement. Paddy just gets himself up, shakes, acts like it never happened and finds himself a flatter patch of grass to roll on.

Paddy's dip and drying complete, I clip his lead on and we trundle over the bridge to the airport field. Half way across, another light aircraft flies directly over our heads to land which is cool to witness. We continue on to the end of the field and I'm still always hopeful the polecats will be there again but sadly they are not so we make our way back. Paddy has another splash in the river on the return journey and I laugh out loud as he, once again, rolls down the bank trying to dry himself. Again, he tries to style out his mishap and casually strolls off with me giggling behind. I wonder if he'll remember where he left the ball. Then, as soon as we reach the railway crossing, he's desperate to get across and his tail starts to wag as he spots his ball on the other side of the style. I let him through and he pounces, picks up his ball and canters off, exuding happiness. I follow on behind, smiling and looking forward to another day spent with Kris and this goof-ball.

MONDAY 30TH AUGUST 2021
9AM : 15 DEGREES C.

Today is Bank Holiday Monday so I enjoyed a nice lay in and leisurely breakfast with the rain coming down outside. I've donned my coat and wellies but the rain stops just as we're about to head out of the gate- what luck! It's pretty mild too. We make our way up to the cricket ground and then out across the sheep field. We've not been this way for a couple of weeks. I'm grateful for my wellies as I trudge through the sodden grass towards the rickety wooden gate on the far side of the field. Along the path leading to the back of the lakes I notice lots of blackberries ripening nicely on the bushes. Around the corner, we join the side of the river which has recently been dredged out (this happens twice per year to all the rivers round here). Reeds and sludge are now piled up on the river bank and not smelling particularly pleasant. The river looks much better for it though and now looks significantly wider! Further up this path I spot a perfectly intact, bright white duck egg. I can only imagine it has been stolen by some animal and left here. It reminds me of the conversation I had with my brother just yesterday. He had told me that he had found some chicken eggs in his garden, buried amongst the plants. I shared how we had something similar in our garden with duck eggs being buried in planters. I had suspected it was the work of a stoat or maybe there are other animals that steal eggs. I wonder if foxes do it as this egg is on the path very close to their dens.

There are lots of fishermen out by the lakes today, clearly making the most of their Bank Holiday. I've never really understood the appeal of fishing myself, it just seems so boring. Although, saying that, I can appreciate the peacefulness/serenity of the activity- just sat there by the water all day. I don't think it's for me though. At the end of this path we go through the metal gate and out into the field. I hope the corn field up ahead has been cut as last time I came this way it was very overgrown on what should be the footpath through the middle of it and, with the rain we've had this morning, it would result in me getting soaked. Now we've reached it, it becomes clear that it has not been cut but we continue on regardless and, actually, it's not as bad as I'd expected. I've got my lightweight walking trousers on too so at least they'll dry off quickly and the rest of the day looks set to be really nice weather.

Out of the overgrown corn field, we enter the corn field which has been cut, making for much easier walking. The clearing out of the rivers has also meant there are now more opportunities for Paddy to get a drink as he can get down the bank where more water is now exposed. Having just had a good drink, he is now having a lovely time rolling around in the grass and I laugh at his glee. The water in the river here is not very deep but looks so peaceful. There is a small bird, going in the same direction as us, flitting from bush to bush on the riverbank. I wonder if it's a wren but it doesn't look quite small enough. Lower down, on the surface of the water, there are lots of patches of what I assume are mosquitoes. There must be six or eight swarms of them on the water that I've passed along this stretch. I just hope they stay down there and don't come up to feast on Paddy and me!

As per usual, we're on our own out here- there are no other people around. I turn 360 degrees and can see Lydd church in the distance and the houses, farm buildings to my right and Brett Aggregates in front. It's so nice to just be out her, not coming across any other people and all I can hear are birds, the wind blowing the grasses at the side of the river and the swishing of my walking trousers (the latter of which annoys Kris- he says he can hear me coming a mile off! They're very comfortable though). Paddy has already made his way down the next footpath, even though he knows he is supposed to wait at the end for me, so I call him back to try again. There is no response to my calls and no sign of him as I make my way down the path. Thankfully he appears as I near the end. My intention to take him back to the start of the path to get a proper "wait" is forgotten as I catch sight of a plant I've not noticed before. I assume it's a wildflower. It has a thin, pink flower head, long leaves and is no more than about 40cm tall. I take a photo of it and will look it up when I get home. It's very pretty though and I notice more of it dotted around me. The more I look, the more I notice that there are actually lots of wildflowers here. In addition to these pink flowers there is purple vetch, the yellow dandelion-head type plants (I really need to identify them!), possibly yellow vetch too. I definitely need to improve my identification skills. Plus there are purple thistles. It looks beautiful! Lastly, I notice the wild carrot and, now that some of it has finished flowering, left behind are these lovely seed heads. I do know I've identified these correctly as I was watching Gardeners World the other day and the legend that is Monty Don was showing us these. As I look at one more closely I see there is a spider living in the middle of it, having spun a little web. Much to my delight and surprise, the next one I look at has a ladybird living in it! I stop to take some photos and reflect on how wonderful it is that nature uses what is available. This is why gardeners are encouraged to leave seed heads etc. and not be too quick to cut everything back as soon as it's finished flowering.

We're now making our way around the field which was the blue carpet of flowering linseed but it's now finished and turned a gorgeous bronze colour, contrasting beautifully with the green grass and oaty coloured grasses. I imagine the seeds are now almost ready to harvest. Upon inspection I see that the plants are laden with small round seed heads. I pick one off the plant and crush it between my fingertips, revealing the individual brown seeds which are identical to the ones I buy to have in my breakfast! It's incredibly satisfying to see this and appreciate, first hand, how something I enjoy eating is grown. Further on, I've come across a big patch of plantain and take note of its location so I can come back and forage it at a later date.

I spot some more of the pink wildflowers amongst the grass and think how lovely it is that so many of these wildflowers are still blooming this late in the summer, providing happy 'pop's of colour. I've enjoyed today's walk immensely. It's been nice, being a Bank Holiday, not having to rush back for anything and just having the time to stop and explore these different plants. In fact, I've now just noticed another which I stop to look at more closely. The leaves look like mint and, following a rub of a leaf between my fingers, I'm delighted to discover that it smells minty too! There are purple flowers up the stem, between the leaves- yet another one for me to photograph and attempt to identify later. It has certainly been a walk for new discoveries- all of which could have so easily been missed if I was rushing.

Apple crumble

Ingredients:

- *2 large cooking apples*
- *120g plain flour*
- *60g butter*
- *60g golden caster sugar*
- *Porridge oats (optional)*

Method:

1. *Peel, core and chop the apples.*
2. *Stew the apple in a saucepan with a few tablespoons of water for 5-6 minutes, then add a couple of teaspoons of sugar and transfer to a dish.*
3. *Rub together the flour and butter to form breadcrumbs, then stir in the sugar (could also add some porridge oats here for a crunchier topping).*
4. *Tip the crumble mix over the apple. Spread it out in an even layer but don't firm it down.*
5. *Cook for 25 minutes at gas mark 5.*

Variations:

- *Apple could be swapped for plums/peaches/ apricots or blackberries added too.*
- *Cinnamon and mixed spice are a nice addition to the apple*

SEPTEMBER

SUNDAY 12TH SEPTEMBER 2021
8AM : 14 DEGREES C.

Even before drawing back the curtains this morning I could tell it was going to be a beautiful day as the early rays of sunshine were streaming through the gap where the curtains hadn't quite met. Kris isn't here this weekend, he's gone away, so I'm making the most of the gorgeous weather by doing the long walk with Paddy today.

We walk up, past the church, towards the cricket ground. I feel there is something really special about September mornings. The light is just beautiful and there's a definite chill in the air now but it feels fresh. I was contemplating putting a jumper on to come out but just stuck with a t-shirt as I know that in about 20 minutes I'll be warm. As I look across to my right at the large trees, the sunlight appears dappled on all of the leaves and there are some jackdaws hopping about in the branches. To my left, the leaves of the trees have turned a silvery colour and look incredible against the backdrop of the bright blue sky.

At the cricket ground, Paddy's poo bag safely deposited in the bin, he is delighted as we turn and head across the road. I don't think he was expecting us to go this way this morning. Along this path, adjacent to the road, I notice there are now rose hips- big, red and oval, accompanying the blackberries. Further on, we reach the sharp corner where the footpath goes across the field. I don't know what has happened here but the fence and style have all been knocked down- perhaps a lorry reversed into it? Regardless of what happened, it has proven advantageous for us as we can now just walk straight into the field and Paddy doesn't have to try to squeeze under the fence! This is the field where potatoes had been planted and the plants have now all gone over so I imagine the farmer will soon be harvesting the potatoes. We make our way along the footpath which goes straight across the middle of this field and I notice just how still it is this morning. There is hardly any wind so the wind turbines are pretty static in the distance- there is just one of them turning very slowly- so I don't think they will be generating much power today.

At the border of the field I climb over the style and Paddy leaps over the fence as there is no provision made for dogs to pass through. There are sheep out here so I have Paddy beside me on a short lead. I think they must be this year's lambs- they look fairly young- and many are enjoying the shade under the large solitary tree at the edge of the field. It's fortunate that it is so flat where we live as I can see two lots of cows in the distance- one herd of dairy and the other beef. Thankfully I can tell they are not going to be in any of the fields we're walking through which is very reassuring!

At the corner of the next field where we exit onto the lane it is very overgrown. I get the impression the farmer doesn't really want walkers coming through this field but, well, tough luck as it's a public right of way! I untie the bailer twine which fastens the metal gates together, let Pads through first and then attempt to keep hold of him in this long grass whilst simultaneously re-tying the twine to the gates. Not an easy feat but I succeed and we head up the lane which, thankfully, is very quiet this morning. As Paddy pulls to the side for a wee, I notice a white butterfly flapping about panicking (can butterflies panic? I imagine they can) as it is caught in a cobweb. Once Pads has finished his wee I ask him to wait as I try to untangle the delicate butterfly from the cobweb. In my hands, I can see it is mainly white with some black spots- very pretty. I manage to gently pull off the last of the cobwebs from the butterfly's body and then open up my hands, watching as it flutters away. I'm pleased to have, hopefully, saved this butterfly's life and it can now continue pollinating which is so important.

We turn left off the road and onto a wide track where I let Paddy off his lead and we make our way up, alongside the river. In the distance I can see a tractor and some machinery out in one of the fields, possibly cutting the last crop. Most of the crops round here have now been harvested though- the linseed, the corn (I say corn but it could have been wheat or barley- I'm not sure I know the difference). All around now are stacks of hay and straw all baled up and I think how much I like September. I'm really not sure what my favourite season is for walking but September is lovely because you can still have really nice, warm mornings but there is a slight chill in the air, giving a fresh feel. Plus, the light in September just feels a bit magical. However, I do also like Spring because, after Winter, it's so nice to start to feel the warmth of the sun again, see the Spring flowers appearing everywhere and it's just an exciting and hopeful time of year. Conversely, I do actually quite like Winter though- when you get a cold, frosty morning and I can wrap up in my coat, gloves and scarf, there's a beautiful blue sky overhead, it's crisp and fresh and my feet are crunching over frozen ground. Then there's Summer and I love being able to just come out in shorts and a t-shirt. So I guess the upshot of this is that, actually, I like walking all year round! Thankfully, I seem able to appreciate the joys that each new season brings.

We reach the ridge where I like to stop and scan the 360 degrees around me. I can see Lydd church, New Romney church, the North Downs towards Ashford, over towards Camber and the hills of Rye in the distance. There is nobody around and this is one of my favourite things about where we live and the places I get to walk. Predominantly it's just me and Paddy, out and about, immersed in nature. Down in the river below us I can see two swans, the feathers on the riverbank evidence of where they nested last night. There are butterflies all around, enjoying the last of the wildflowers and I spot one that looks like the one I untangled from the cobweb. I'm doubtful it's the same one though as we've walked quite a distance since then and I'm not sure butterflies can fly that fast! I can also hear the frogs in the river making their noisy calls to one another. Now, up ahead, a large bird takes flight from the stone bridge. It must be a bird of prey of some description- the wingspan looks over a meter- and it flies off down the length of the river.

Having now crossed the stone bridge, we make our way down the edge of the field where, underfoot, it is really hard and dry. I can't really remember the last time we had rain. It's certainly been a long time since we've had a wet walk. At the corner of this field we exit onto the footpath which narrows between the hedgerows. It is stunning down here- there are at least fifteen of those white butterflies with black spots flitting about (they seem to like the wildflowers that are down here) and there is the blackberry hedgerow. It's just a lovely little haven here. Further on, there are some hawthorn trees which I notice are now adorned with red berries. However, it is a bird in the distance which steals my attention. It is large and white which makes me think it's a swan but it looks more slender. I've called Paddy to me as I don't want him to chase it- particularly if it is a swan as they never seem to have a very fast getaway! The bird has just flown off and I now think it's a heron but I'm confused because it was definitely white, not grey like a heron. It was as white as a swan but its silhouette and the way it flew was heron-like. Is there such thing as a white heron? Or perhaps it's a different bird entirely.

The sun is beating down now so I'm pleased I put some sunscreen on my face this morning and that we came out fairly early. It's been a wonderful start to our Sunday though and I'm looking forward to a restful remainder of the day.

THURSDAY 16TH SEPTEMBER 2021
7:25AM : 11 DEGREES C.

As soon as I walk out of the house this morning I notice the drop in temperature. It feels very fresh and crisp and, as we make our way along past the houses, I notice my hands are feeling cold. I pull down the sleeves of my jumper in response and tuck my fingers up inside to try to keep them warm. It's the first time this season that I've actually felt cold but I know it won't be long before the sun comes through and I get warm walking anyway. As we reach the church I see that it is shrouded in fog- there's a really thick blanket of fog everywhere this morning. On the path up ahead there is not much visibility at all.

At the cricket ground there is nobody else about and it almost feels quite eerie in the fog. I suppose this fog and the drop in temperature is typical of a September morning though. We head along the wide track towards the fishing lakes and, as we come through the kissing gate, I notice all of the spiders webs along the path ahead. They are so much more noticeable in the fog as all the little beads of moisture cover the threads and make them look quite beautiful. The spiders webs are all the way across the path from the hedgerow to the fence so I can tell I'm the first person to walk along here this morning as they're still intact. It feels like I'm constantly going through the winning tape at the end of a race as I keep breaking through all of these webs. The worst thing is when they're at head height and you don't see them and end up with threads of cobweb stuck to your face, so fine that you then can't get them off properly. At the end of this footpath it's got rather overgrown again. On the left there are brambles from the blackberry bushes and, on the right, there is gorse but the two are now starting to meet in the middle so it's a squeeze to navigate through. Now I've got my hair snagged in a bramble so have to take a few steps backwards in an attempt to untangle myself.

Even just in the ten minutes or so of walking this section, the sun has started to burn through the fog and I can now see some blue sky and feel the heat of the sun on my skin, its touch most definitely welcome. Looking behind me, I see that the church is still hidden behind a wall of fog though. It won't be long before the sun has worked its magic and erased all of the fog, I'm sure, as it looks set to be another very nice day. There is hardly any wind this morning so it's very still, with hardly a ripple on the fishing lakes. I stop for a moment and watch the mist rising off the lake and a swan gliding along serenely. All I can hear is some birds tweeting in the hedgerow and some of the jackdaws "caw"ing in the distance.

Paddy is waiting for me at the end of this path. I climb over the style and give him the "okay" to squeeze through the gap. He immediately darts off to find some sheep poo to eat before I call him on. I then stop in my tracks to look at some trees out here. One has lots of hawthorn berries on but I notice another which, previously I'd thought was also hawthorn due to the blossom, is actually a plum. It is now adorned with lots of big, yellow plums! I would very much like to pick some but the tree is down a bank and behind a barbed wire fence so is not very easily accessible. It's interesting that I've only just discovered this though, now that it's in fruit. I'm disappointed I can't reach it as there is a lot of fruit on it but we must continue on our way. As I walk away I notice that there are also lots of blackberries tangled up the side of the tree. There's a very tasty blackberry and plum crumble right there waiting to be made! There are sometimes sheep in this field but I see no sign of them today so keep Paddy off lead. He was very content just mooching about whilst I was eyeing up the plum tree.

We'll soon reach the time of year for foraging sloes. I know my Dad has already managed to find some to pick, ready for making sloe gin. I did manage to pick a load last year but it was when I was out running so in order to get back to that location it'll either require a run or a very long walk. Anyway, it would be nice to pick some more as I did enjoy the sloe gin last year and it makes great Christmas gifts too! The fog has now lifted even more and I can now make out the church. In this next field there are lots more spiders' webs and they really do look beautiful amongst the grasses with the morning sunlight now coming through.

We're now heading towards the farmhouse where we are usually greeted by Jessie the Border Collie. She normally hears us coming and starts barking but as soon as I call out "Hey, Jessie!" she knows it's us and comes out onto the path all wiggly for a tummy rub.

She wants to give Paddy a sniff but he never shows any interest in her at all. It's almost like he sees her as an interruption to his walk and he needs to get on with his important explorations. I always make sure I stop and say hello though as she's such a lovely dog. As I look down the river I see some swans and their cygnets all sitting on the riverbank cleaning themselves. There are four cygnets which is a great success for the parents.

As we walk down the farm drive towards the road, rabbits dart across and into their burrows, causing Paddy's ears to prick up and eyes to fixate on where they've disappeared to. We turn left onto the footpath and it is covered with big, black slugs- huge ones, almost the size of sausages! We pick our way along, trying to avoid them and their slimy trails. Although it's parallel to the main road, this footpath feels quite tucked away as the large hedge acts as a screen from the road. I notice some more blackberries along here and realise I've still not actually foraged any yet this year- I really must. I enjoy the peace and quiet along here before we head into the high street and through the town to get back home.

MONDAY 27TH SEPTEMBER 2021
7:20AM : 16 DEGREES C.

The sky is cloudy this morning, there is quite a bit of wind and it's forecast to rain so I'm wearing my thin raincoat without a jumper underneath. At the end of our close, we turn left and walk along past all the houses before emerging on the patch of scrubland. Paddy always stops here to go to the toilet before we then turn the corner, cross the road and make our way down over the railway line. We then cross the road again to join the footpath between a couple of houses. On our left there is a paddock which is home to a gaggle of geese who are strutting about and honking, seemingly demanding their breakfast. In the paddock behind them there are some horses and, on our right, there are two lovely black Shetland ponies. As we walk down here the tree line ahead catches my attention. I'm not sure if they are beech trees but all of the leaves have turned silver and, where it's windy today, there is just this swaying and shimmering of silver which looks beautiful.

We cross the little bridge and I notice that there is not really water below, more like green sludge. Paddy is waiting at the gate for me and I pop him on his lead. I can't see any cows in the field at the moment but there is a chance they could be round the corner. Consequently, I'm checking over my shoulder every few steps to check if they're round the bend. We then reach the point where I can see the whole field and I spot the herd of cows- thankfully a safe distance away from us! I feel reassured to see them so far in the distance, contentedly grazing, and we reach the next gate. For a long time this section of the walk had been completely overgrown- I'd reported it to the council but nothing seemed to happen and it was becoming almost impassable. I therefore decided to take matters into my own hands and, one morning, came armed with secateurs and snipped my way through. It took me a good twenty minutes but it has made a huge difference and I can now walk through here with ease.

It is now starting to feel quite autumnal which I'm enjoying. There are blackberries in the hedgerow and all along here there are hawthorn berries, round and red. The sky is looking moody above, adding to the Autumn-vibe. The only slight anomaly is that it's still very warm. We're out in the open now and make our way along the side of the field, being battered by the wind as we go up towards the farm.

Along the lane I notice that all of the Autumn colours are starting to show- the trees are turning yellow and bronze which looks lovely. At my feet on the road, I enjoy shuffling my way through those leaves that have already fallen. The rustling noise is incredibly satisfying, accompanied by the swaying of the branches above. Paddy is waiting at the railway crossing up ahead. I'm so pleased that is something we taught him- to wait at the crossing until we give him the "okay" to cross. It's worth pointing out that the railway lines we have round here are very rarely used and, on those few occasions there is a train, it's a very slow-moving goods train going to or from Dungeness Power Station so that's why we allow Paddy to approach the crossings like this. Further on, there are more blackberries, hawthorn berries and rose hips. I'm a little disappointed I've still not got round to picking any this year but my thoughts are interrupted by the barking of the dogs at the house we're now passing. They always bark when we walk past but Paddy is so used to it now that he just trots on past, barely glancing. Interestingly, we did look at buying the house next door to this one but it needed so much work doing to it- the floor was wonky and there was a dead mouse in the middle of the living room floor when we viewed it- so we decided it was too big a project for us. Whoever did buy it has done a good job though as it now looks fantastic so kudos to them for taking it on!

I clip Paddy's lead on as we approach the main road and we continue round past the field where the sheep are looking a little perturbed by the rain which is now coming down heavily. Combined with the wind, it's really quite unpleasant! At the sharp corner, Paddy often wants to cut through into the cricket field but I usually ignore his request and continue on the road due to it being overgrown. Today, however, I see the foliage has died back enough for us to get through so, much to Pad's delight, we do. Rather unsurprisingly, nobody else is out in the cricket ground in this rain. As we head back down the road towards the church, I spot one other dog walker looking fairly miserable with their hood up. The closer we get to home, the heavier the rain gets and we are getting absolutely drowned. It will be a case of drying Pads off (with at least two large towels) and then me towel-drying off and getting a complete change of clothes when we get home. Autumn has definitely arrived!

Plum & ginger chutney

Ingredients:

- 750g plums
- 50g fresh ginger
- 2 onions
- 125g sultanas
- 1 tbsp cinnamon
- 1tbsp mixed spice
- 400g demerara sugar
- 450ml distilled white vinegar

Method:

1. De-stone the plums and cut them into quarters, then add to a large preserving pan.
2. Peel and dice the ginger, then add to the pan.
3. Peel and chop the onion, then add to the pan.
4. Add the sultanas, cinnamon, mixed spice, sugar and vinegar to the pan. Give it a good stir and bring it to the boil.
5. Reduce the heat and simmer for 1 – 2 hours, stirring frequently. The mixture will become thick and glossy. When you can drag a wooden spoon across the bottom of the pan to leave a channel that doesn't immediately fill with liquid, you know it's ready.
6. Transfer to sterilised jars and allow to cool completely before putting on the lids.

Sloe gin

Ingredients:

- *450g sloes*
- *225g granulated sugar*
- *70cl gin*

Method:

1. *Prick each sloe a couple of times with a skewer.*
2. *Add sloes to a Kilner jar (no more than 2/3 full- use 2 jars if necessary). Add the sugar and, lastly, the gin.*
3. *Shake the jar once every day or two for the first few weeks to ensure the sugar mixes in.*
4. *Leave for 3 to 6 months, then strain and bottle.*

Tip:

You can re-use the sloes from the gin to make 'Nelson's Blood'! Just add 70cl of ruby port to them and leave for 3 months then strain and bottle.

OCTOBER

WEDNESDAY 13TH OCTOBER 2021
7AM : 6 DEGREES C.

This morning is the coldest it's been so far this Autumn. When I let Paddy out into the garden first thing I could really feel that bitterness to the air. Consequently, I've got my gloves on for the first time in months, plus my headband to cover my ears and I'm very grateful for them because it really is quite chilly!

It's a very clear morning with just a few clouds and we begin our walk by heading out of our close and turning left. As we walk along past the houses there is this noise that sounds like a big gust of wind but it's odd because everything around me is still. I look up and coming overhead is a murmuration of starlings- hundreds of them. Obviously the noise I heard was the combined flapping of their wings, creating that rushing noise. It's such a spectacle to see and I stand and watch, transfixed, as they fly off into the distance. Once they're out of sight we continue on and, at the end of this road, next to the last house there is a creeping plant which has turned the most beautiful shade of red. I can see the transitioning of the leaves. Some are still green, some orange and others this vivid red which just looks stunning. We make our way up the footpath and Paddy always stops here to go to the toilet. Unfortunately, yesterday Pads had a bit of an upset stomach and, this morning, there is still an element of Mr Whippy present so it's not the easiest to clean up...

We cross the main road and then the railway line as, today, we're heading over to the area of scrubland near the entrance to the airport. Out here I notice that the ground in some of the more exposed areas is looking a bit silvery so I think we probably had our first slight frost of the Autumn last night. I need to deposit the poo bag in the bin which is up ahead and I'm convinced Paddy knows what I mean when I say "We've got to go to the bin" because he then very much leads me over to the bin and stands beside it whilst I toss the bag in.

This is the area we come to because Paddy loves to do digging over here. There are absolutely loads of rabbit holes. It's just an area of scrubland but quite a few dog walkers use it and it just makes quite a nice, shorter walk, taking about 50 minutes which is what I need this morning as I've got to get to work early. Paddy is currently shoulder-deep in a hole. He has to stay on the lead out here because it's next to the main road but he doesn't seem to mind that, he's just content with doing lots of digging. He does often get absolutely filthy and, occasionally, we leave here with him making funny noises due to the fact he's got dirt up his nose. However, digging is a natural behaviour for dogs and this is a suitable place for him to do some so I don't mind it. He never actually encounters any rabbits- he can just smell them and enjoys the digging! I look across the road to my right and notice the mist coming up from the ground. To my left, looking out towards the coast, the sun is just rising. When we first came out this morning I could just see the orangey, pinky hue in the sky but I now see the full sun, a big golden ball, above the horizon and it looks stunning. Seeing it somehow makes me feel that little bit warmer, even though the ground around me is silver. The sky is blue today and I notice the many aeroplane trails across it in random directions, as well as groups of birds flying between the trees.

It's time for me to move Paddy on as he's been digging in this particular hole for quite some time and I know he'll want to investigate other areas before we make our way back home.

MONDAY 25TH OCTOBER 2021
7:25AM : 13 DEGREES C.

It's already raining quite a bit as we prepare to go out this morning so I fully 'waterproof up', minus my baseball cap (I don't think I need to go to that extent) and we leave the house. Paddy isn't bothered by the rain at all.

We make our way out of the close and turn left, along past the houses, to join the little footpath that leads up behind the Police station and nursery. Then we cross the main road and head down over the railway crossing and up the other side to cross the road again. Just recently, Paddy has been a bit funny at this point as he seems to want to go and look down all the rabbit holes on the area of scrubland rather than crossing over and doing the cow walk. However, once we're on the cow walk, he's absolutely fine and loving it. I just have to stop him from lunging ahead and make it clear that we are, in fact, crossing the road. This morning, however, there seems to be a lot of traffic so we're stood here waiting to cross for some time and there are a lot of puddles, resulting in sprays of water coming up as cars pass by but, thankfully, we're standing just far enough back that we avoid getting splattered!

Finally we make it across the road and head down the footpath between a couple of houses and past the paddocks where, this morning, the Shetland ponies are out. I then notice a flash of orange and see a fox jumping one of the paddock fences. Thankfully Paddy hasn't seen it but I'm not going to risk letting him off lead just yet like I usually do as I know he'll pick up the scent of it and will be off tracking. Just as we reach the end of this path, I see Paddy's nose go down, scenting and he's getting increasingly animated so clearly he has picked up the scent of the fox. Hopefully the fox will stay hidden away.

We come through the gate and out into the open field and, thankfully, there are no cows in sight at all today. As I look back over my shoulder (to check that there are no cows hiding round the corner!) I see the fox pop out from the undergrowth and it stops in its tracks and looks straight at me. Thankfully Paddy is more focussed on the route ahead so has not noticed. However, in a mad leap of faith, I gesture at the fox to go back into the undergrowth so it can remain hidden whilst Paddy and I get across the field. After a few moments the fox does go back through the hedge, whether under its own volition or as a result of my gesturing I don't know but I'm pleased it's safe!

We pass through the gate on the other side of the field and, after just a few paces, Paddy shoots off, sprinting along the path after what I assume is a rabbit. I continue pootling on my own and consider how, at the moment, it's easy to look around and see everything as a bit drab. All of the lovely silvery leaves which were present at the start of Autumn have fallen and the remaining leaves are just brown. On the face of it, everything just looks a bit...dead. However, when I look closer at things there is still a lot of beauty to be found. On some of the branches there are raindrops which look like strings of pearls, glistening in the morning light. There are a lot of hawthorn bushes along here and they are currently laden with red berries which look lovely.

I stand and wait for a while as Paddy does his usual digging in this exposed area of ground. After a few minutes I call his name so we can continue on our way and, just behind me, a pheasant shoots up. It must have been there a while, just unbeknown to me, and upon hearing my voice it manically flapped its wings and flew off, scaring the life out of me! Composure regained, Paddy and I carry on down the edge of the cow field.

I thought I was going to get too warm in all my waterproofs but actually, at the moment, it's not too bad. The rain has stopped completely now though so I've removed my hood and, looking around, the sky looks pretty promising. There are some grey clouds around, more so over the coast, but inland looks fairly clear. Hopefully we'll at least get back home without too much more rain.

At the gate into the next field there are loads of teasels and they've got really tall- many of them are above my head! They almost have a cactus-like shape to them and are a gorgeous chocolatey –brown colour, dried out and very pretty. After admiring the teasels, we climb through the fence (there is a handy big gap meaning I don't have to worry about undoing the chain on the gate) and make our way up the next field.

I'm standing in the farmyard waiting for Paddy as he's intensely sniffing some grass further back. I can hear the quite soothing sound of chickens clucking away in the barn. Content with his sniffing, Paddy then joins me and we head out onto the lane. Along here, a lot of the leaves have fallen, leaving the trees looking quite bare but providing me with the satisfaction of kicking my way through the leaves. Over to my left, a rabbit hops through the fence and a pheasant flies up behind it- possibly the same one from earlier. We cross the railway line and, further on, pass the cottages. The fields to my right appear to have a one meter high wall of mist coming up from the ground. I'm snapped out of this observation by the barking of the dogs in the cottage though. They rush out and jump at the fence, barking at us as we pass by. Thankfully Paddy shows very little interest (he's used to this routine by now) and just continues trotting along, looking a bit bemused at why they continue to bark. This morning I smile as I notice that, because the dogs are both Staffies with very thin fur, they are sporting lovely little cosy jumpers to keep them warm!

At the end of the lane I pop Paddy back on his lead ready to walk along the road, past the cricket ground and church to get back home. It looks fairly promising that the rain has finished and the sky is blue above me so hopefully we'll return home in the dry.

NOVEMBER

TUESDAY 2ND NOVEMBER 2021
2PM : 10 DEGREES C.

It has turned into a beautiful day- really sunny, blue sky and some white, fluffy clouds. It has warmed up considerably since this morning but you can still definitely feel it's November. I've enjoyed my warm bowl of home-made soup for lunch and am now heading out with Paddy.

We leave our close, cross the road and go up between a couple of houses where, because it's shaded, it's really chilly! The sun just doesn't ever get in this little alleyway. I'm pleased to come out onto the main road and into the warmth of the sunshine. We walk along the pavement for a while before crossing the road and going up between some more houses to bring us out onto the Rype.

We pass the play park where a man is sitting, watching his two young children playing on the swings and slide, their joy evident in their squeals and laughter. I can see there are three other dog walkers out here today so I will keep Pads on his lead just to be safe as he does have a tendency to want to go and say hello to other dogs (or hump them...) As Paddy stops to sniff something I notice there are loads of spiders' webs on the grass. It's only when we cross over onto the other side of the Rype that I notice the full extent of the spiders' work though. The webs totally cover the whole of the Rype. It must be the way that the sunlight is landing which is making them more visible and it's sort of shining through them. It's just so odd to see! I stop to take a photo although I'm not sure it will do it justice.

We cross back over to the first side of the Rype and walk along the tree line ready to leave. Paddy starts trying to wipe his head with his paw as, where he's been sniffing, he's now got spiders' webs all over his face so I use my hand to try to remove them for him. As I look down to do this, I notice that his feet and my walking boots are absolutely covered in webs too! I'll have to try to clean them off when we get home.

We walk along by the road and then pick up the short footpath which takes us past the cemetery. I'm feeling so content right now with a tummy full of home-made soup, the sun shining down on me, out with Paddy on this lovely fresh day with blue sky above me. I just really enjoy getting out at lunchtime with Paddy as it nicely breaks up my working day- it's great to get away from the computer and phone and just get out in the fresh air for some exercise.

Having passed the cemetery, we come back out on the main road and I wait to see which way Paddy wants to go- back down the cold alleyway or round the corner, past the vets. As I suspected (because he's not found any 'treasure' aka litter/sticks that he wants to get home quickly with), he takes us round past the vets. Here, he stands for ages, sniffing as there are always so many smells from the stream of visiting pets. After a few minutes I call him on and we head back home ready for me to clean off my boots (and Paddy's feet!).

FRIDAY 12TH NOVEMBER 2021
7AM : 11 DEGREES C.

This morning we've headed out fairly early as I'm aiming to start work at 8am. We're going to do the airport walk so head out of our close, walk up past the vets and then cross the road to make our way down past the cemetery. I notice that the flowers in everyone's gardens are really coming to their end now and everything is starting to look very 'wintery' and bare. As we walk along the main road, with the cemetery now on our right, over the hedge I see that someone has decorated one of the memorials with pumpkins and cotton wool cobwebs which I think is a nice touch.

We now make our way out into the field and there is no sign of anyone else out here as usual. There are no sheep out here at the moment either so I let Paddy off his lead. The sun is just peeking up from the horizon and it looks beautiful. There is something truly mesmerising about the sunrise and seeing it always fills me with so much hope and optimism for the day ahead. With every sunrise there is opportunity for a fresh start. I watch as the sun slowly, inch by inch, makes its ascent. Over my head, there are lots of sea birds flying, along with some starlings happily chittering, and it's just a really pleasant morning. The sky is blue and dotted with just a few white clouds.

We go through the gap into the next field where there are potatoes growing, much to Paddy's delight! His nose is firmly to the ground, trying to sniff out and snuffle some. Meanwhile, I walk along and get lost in my thoughts but am then brought back to the present moment by the sound of all the grasses bordering the dyke to my left, swaying in the breeze. Then I notice that the sun is now emitting this glorious golden glow which, cast on the swaying grasses, just looks absolutely stunning. I appreciate that, right now, in this moment, I'm out in nature and it is truly beautiful. This peaceful, mindful moment then comes to an abrupt end with Paddy chomping on yet another potato so I call him back onto the path and we continue on our way.

We're now into the next field, having just crossed over the little wooden bridge, and are making our way across. The sun has now risen even higher and I notice it's almost in line with the water tower. A keen photographer, no doubt, would capture an amazing image of this with the sun looking like a fiery ball on the top of the water tower. I have neither a fancy camera or the necessary skills to achieve this but I take a snapshot in my mind and then we cross the railway line and traverse the style into the next field.

Out here, Paddy has found some nice grass to chomp on. I swear it's like a second breakfast when he comes out for a walk! He then trots off down to the riverbank and a cacophony ensues with a swan flapping about. I rush over just as the swan is swimming away to safety. I suspect, to be fair, that they probably both made each other jump. Paddy just went to get a drink and was surprised by the swan, who was equally surprised to see Paddy! With the swan now further down the river and Paddy's drink complete, we head over the bridge and into the airfield, Paddy firmly on lead. There are still quite a few mushrooms out here, including some of those enormous, dinner-plate sized ones. I still can't help but hope that, when we get to the end, we'll see the polecats. Sadly, they are not to be seen today though. I think that must have just been one very fortunate occasion where we saw them previously but I'm that kind of person that always holds on to hope and optimism.

We make our way back over the bridge and I release Paddy from his lead once more. He enjoys another drink from the river and then a good mooch about on the bank. All around our area, the dykes have recently been dredged out, leaving all the reeds and vegetation piled up on the riverbanks so Paddy is clambering over it all and having a good sniff about to see what other delicacies he might be able to find. The sun is now fully up in the sky and it looks like it's going to be a very nice day.

On our return across the fields, I notice that the one to our left is full of swans. We often find that around here on the Marsh- loads of swans out in the fields. It's probably partly due to the fact that we're very close to Dungeness Nature Reserve here as well, so I think they come over from the lakes over there. There must be things they eat in the fields as they all look busy feeding. As we walk along here I can see Paddy air-scenting and looking across. I don't think it's the swans he's interested in but he's clearly caught the scent of something and starts to get more excited and begins to pick up speed. Thankfully he responds absolutely perfectly when I tell him "no" and to "come back on the path"- I'm very impressed! This impeccable behaviour us somewhat short lived as he now proceeds to grab a potato to eat. I shout "spit it out!" - I can't quite remember how that phrase came about but Paddy does definitely know what it means and he duly spits out the potato which I then hurl over the hedgerow, out of his reach. Paddy then trots merrily on his way with me following behind.

TUESDAY 16TH NOVEMBER 2021
7:10AM : 10 DEGREES C.

I think it's going to be fairly mild today so I've opted to come out without my gloves but I do have my coat on as the sky is looking a bit grey. I don't think it's going to rain but it's best to be prepared (that's the Girl Guide in me!). As we walk out of our close we meet one of our neighbours who is returning from walking their dog so we stop for a moment for a chat. Another neighbour then passes us in their car, giving a cheery wave. I feel very fortunate to live where we do as it's a very friendly community around here, with everyone looking out for each other. "Hello"s complete, we begin our walk and Paddy seems very keen this morning- he's pulling on the lead rather a lot. It might be because he needs the toilet so I'm hoping he'll slow down after that!

We make our way up towards the cricket ground and another dog walker we know passes by in their car, giving us a wave. I automatically reciprocate the wave but, due to holding Paddy on his lead in one hand and a full poo bag in the other, I fear all I've really done is waved poo at them. They're a dog owner though; they'll relate and understand my intent! When we reach the cricket ground it's deserted. Often there are a couple of other dog walkers in the field but not this morning which is quite nice. It's very peaceful.

As we come on to the rough track that goes along here a rabbit runs out and its white, cotton tail bobs along as it darts to the side to avoid us. Paddy's ears prick up in response but he's not overly interested. Further up ahead I can see a murmuration of starlings, like a swarm of locusts- it looks absolutely amazing. It is one of those natural spectacles that is simply awe inspiring. The murmuration comes round to the right of me, just thick with birds, and eventually they all land in one of the fields. Ahead though, I notice there are even more starlings, all perched on one of the electricity cables- it's laden with them and causing the cable to be bowing under the combined weight of all of them. As we get closer they all fly off, leaving the cable bouncing up and down.

We're now heading along the footpath with the lakes on our right and it's really peaceful this morning. There is hardly any breeze at all so the water is perfectly still, looking almost like a mirror. As we near the end of this path I need to try to establish where the cows are as, unfortunately, the farmer has now put them out in this next field. I can see them all dotted around out there so I'm not going to be able to go the way I wanted, round past Jessie's farm, but I'm hoping as they're over that way we might be able to just sneak across the top of this field to get out into the big field to the right. As I plan our safe passage I notice some of the gorse is flowering, providing a welcome 'pop' of colour along the otherwise bare path.

We safely manage to cut across the top of the cow field and I plan on just heading up this next field, to the corner, and then heading back. However, I'm a little on edge as, next to the fishing lake, there's a man dressed all in black with his hood up and he is walking towards the area we are heading through. Just this man on his own, no dog or anything else with him and just looking a bit shifty. It's funny how something like this can make you feel so uncomfortable- someone acting a bit unusual and knowing I'm a lady on my own (though with Paddy), kind of in the middle of nowhere. There's nobody else around, that's for sure. I keep Paddy close by me and keep half an eye on the man and am relieved as I see him head back round to the other side of the lake. I still don't know what he was doing but I hope that's the end of it.

With my attention now back on the way ahead I notice a large bird of prey by the electricity pylon. I can't see what it is but watch as it hops about, flapping its big wings. We then turn around and head back the way we came, me hoping that we can get back through before the cows have moved up the field! As we head back, I see a man in the distance but moving in our direction and watch with baited breath as he climbs the style into the field we're in. Thankfully, I then see Jessie the Border collie leaping through the grass and a swish of her white tail which means this is a man I know well and not the suspicious one from earlier! Paddy spots them and sprints off towards them, causing Jessie to do her usual bouncing around and barking, undecided as to whether she's scared or wants to play. Paddy, however, then just walks nonchalantly past, showing no interest at all. Myself and Jessie's owner stop and have a conversation for a while and I share how reassuring it was for me to know he and Jessie had just walked right through the field of cows and the cows clearly hadn't shown any interest at all. He assures me he's walked through them countless times and never had any problems. I try to see this as proof that my fear is unfounded but I still don't think I'll be risking it any time soon! If ever there is an alternative route to avoid cows, I'll take it! I notice Pads has now moved further ahead and is staring at something so I say a hasty goodbye and rush to catch up with him. It can't have been anything that exciting because, as soon as I call him, he sprints straight towards me, almost barrelling into my legs! Nice recall though…

I pop Pads back on his lead as we cut across the cow field and we're now safely back onto the footpath, heading down with the lakes now on the left. I can now see that the shifty man is, in fact, a fisherman, now back on the far side of the lake with his tent and car. Hopefully he was just looking for another potential fishing spot to relocate to but I don't think men understand how their behaviour can make women feel when we're on our own like that. I think it's something men need to be more aware of. If he'd have taken his hood off, called out "good morning" or waited by the water rather than heading towards me, it might have just made me feel a little safer. Anyway, everything turned out alright in the end. We continue our walk, back past the cricket ground and church and head home.

FRIDAY 26TH NOVEMBER 2021
7:10AM : 4 DEGREES C.

The weather forecast for today was drizzle all day but, whilst having my breakfast, I could see it looked dry outside- no signs of precipitation at all! However, given that it's so cold this morning and there's a chance of rain I've put my waterproof trousers on in addition to my coat. The temperature has really dropped this week- it definitely feels like winter now, so I've got my gloves and not quite a hat yet but a woolly head band to cover my ears and that has been just right this week.

We've headed out of our close and turned to go up past the vets. As we cross the road here, Paddy gets incredibly excited, tugging ahead, wagging his tail enthusiastically and 'smiling'. He always tends to have that reaction when we go this way. My suspicion as to why is that, on this walk, there are often potatoes which he delights on finding and eating! As we walk down the road past the cemetery we bump into Ian who is walking his little dog, Ebony. We exchange a few pleasantries- generally weather-related (as is the case with most dog walkers!) and then carry on our way. It's still quite dark this morning- I think the heavy cloud cover is causing it to take longer to brighten up. The street lights are only just starting to turn themselves off as we walk along here. We turn left into the close to go past the play park and then out into the field. As we enter, a whole murmuration of starlings passes over head- there must be thousands of them- and the resulting noise, that "whoosh" of wind as they all flap their wings simultaneously is incredible!

I let Paddy off his lead in this first field and there is nobody else to be seen which is what we like! In the second field there is definitely a crop emerging- from looking at the leaves I think it's potatoes so Paddy will be in his element!

I often find myself singing on this walk as it's so open and there's nobody else around. This morning, I'm singing some Guide campfire songs and thinking how interesting it is that there can be songs you've not sung or even heard in years, yet you're still able to recall all of the words. It's mad and a bit frustrating when random song lyrics cement themselves into your memory yet important information often won't stick! There is quite a breeze this morning so all of the grasses next to the stream are swaying and rustling which is very relaxing. This peaceful moment is interrupted when I notice Paddy is crunching his way through a very large potato so I ask him to "leave it" and then fling it over the other side of the river so that he can't pick it up again on the way back.

We've now come over the little bridge and I call Paddy back to me. Usually he waits at the end of the bridge for me but something clearly caught his attention. Together, we now make our way across the next field. It is very grey today but, thankfully, still remaining dry and I'm certainly not too hot in all my layers so am glad I put them on. We go over the two styles to cross the railway line and head for the river. As I look around me I consider how different everything looks as the seasons change. Several months ago, this field was almost shoulder-height with golden corn swaying in the breeze. Now, however, there are just stumpy bits of corn, a couple of inches tall and everything looks very barren. I'm quickly snapped out of my thoughts by Paddy sprinting off in front and then I notice the lovely big fox jump up onto the wooden bridge and sprint across. Paddy then leaps onto the bridge and dashes across in chase and it all feels very much like a cartoon moment or comedy sketch as I then sprint after Paddy. Thankfully, at the end of the bridge, the fox turns right and into the thick hedgerow, rather than straight across the airfield. I honestly think that, in a flat race, Paddy would have been faster than the fox and therefore caught him so heading for the hedge was a wise move on the fox's part! Paddy sniffs around, trying to work out where the fox has gone, which gives me the opportunity to catch up and get him secured safely back on his lead. Now I notice that Paddy has got a load of burrs in his tail though which clearly he's picked up from the hedgerow so I work my way through teasing them all out before they get too matted in his long fur.

With the burrs successfully removed, we continue up the field and Paddy is really scenting. I imagine the fox came down this way before meeting us. At the end we turn around and make our way back. It's only on our return that I notice a carcass near the bridge and I realise this is what the fox must have been doing when we disturbed it. As I get closer I can see that the carcass is quite a big bird- a bird of prey or seagull perhaps. The feathers don't look right for a seagull though and I think, actually, it could be an owl as the feathers are white and tan and look very soft. After Paddy has had a quick drink from the river we head back over the railway line.

Halfway down the next field, Paddy sniffs excitedly at the ground and starts digging. There is no sign of a rabbit so it must be a mouse or something he can smell as he very intently starts to dig a hole. Rather comically, every time I try to move out of the firing line of the dirt he's flinging between his back legs as he digs, he seems to spin round and direct it at me! He's now got mud all over his face and, where his legs are wet, the dirt is sticking to them so that'll be fun to clean off when we get back home...still, at least he's had an exciting walk!

Sweet potato and orange soup

Ingredients:

- *1 large sweet potato*
- *1 white onion*
- *1 can butter beans*
- *800ml vegetable stock*
- *Zest of 1 small orange*

Method:

1. Chop the sweet potato into 1cm cubes and add to the soup maker.
2. Dice the onion and add to the soup maker.
3. Drain the butter beans and add to the soup maker, along with the vegetable stock.
4. Zest the orange and add it to the soup maker.
5. Blend the soup to a 'smooth' consistency.

Tips:

- If you don't own a soup maker, buy one. Honestly, you won't regret it. Autumn and Winter are made infinitely better by the ease of a soup maker!
- Best enjoyed with a large chunk of thick bread with a generous layer of butter on for dunking.
- You'll likely get 4 servings from this recipe- perfect for a week of easy and nutritious lunches!

DECEMBER

FRIDAY 17TH DECEMBER 2021
7:30AM : 8 DEGREES C.

It's been really enjoyable looking at everyone's Christmas decorations on our walks this month! Obviously, at this time of the day people don't have the lights on but you can still see some houses just absolutely covered in them, with the promise of how magical they'll look when dusk descends. I notice lots of lovely wreaths on people's doors too. I feel like, this year, people have gone all out on decorations because of the pretty much cancelled Christmas we had last year due to Covid. I'm certainly enjoying seeing all these decorations anyway and admire how nice the church looks as we walk past. There is a huge golden star lit up on the top of the tower which you can see for miles around and, out the front, there is a large Christmas tree adorned with bright white twinkling lights.

We walk up the lane towards the cricket ground which, for the past two weeks, has been closed to traffic as there has been work happening on the bridge over the river. It's therefore been really nice walking up here knowing there is no traffic. Following on behind us is the couple with their wriggly Cocker Spaniel, Fin, but there doesn't seem to be any other dog walkers about this morning. In fact, all the while the road has been closed it's been quieter as many people drive up here to walk their dogs. Further along the track I spot the lady with her two Airedale Terriers though. It's quite funny because they always rush over to Paddy to say hello and want to play yet Pads couldn't be more disinterested and just wants to carry on with his sniffing and his walk. It's like he has far more important things to be doing.

I've heard lots of sirens in the distance whilst walking along here and wonder what's going on and where. We make our way through the gate and up the path past the lakes. There is a lot of bird song this morning but, aside from that (and the distant sirens!), everything is silent and still. All of this week has been very mild for the time of year- earlier this week it was 11 degrees in the morning!

We reach the style which leads out into the field and, thankfully, a couple of weeks ago the cows were moved out of here and into the other field and barn, ready for calving. Consequently, I'm very much enjoying not having the worry of encountering the cows! I know it's only a matter of time before they are put back out here with their calves though- and then they'll be even more on alert and feeling protective over their young. I'll make the most of this time while it lasts! Paddy is waiting at the style for me to give him the "okay" and then he'll dive through the gap and attempt to snuffle some rabbit poo before I can catch up with him. On this occasion, I successfully manage to stop him from eating any and we continue across this field, through the gate and head up the side of the next field. Paddy then speeds off ahead of me and, the next thing I know, he's rolling on his back which indicates to me that he has found something suitably rancid to roll in. I rush over and shoo him away but, sure enough, there is something disgusting in the grass (and now on Paddy's back and shoulders). He's going to smell delightful all day!

We continue around this field and I notice some swans flying in the distance. Whilst I'm watching the sky, Paddy catches sight of something up ahead and sprints up the path. I pick up my pace but then see him go through into the next field, towards where I know there are sheep. With my heart starting to pound, I sprint as fast as I can in my wellies, water splashing up my legs as my feet crash through puddles and I try not to turn my ankle over. Thankfully, when I make it out into the next field, Paddy is coming back in my direction, away from the sheep, and I feel a flood of relief. I manage to call him back to me and keep him close as we continue around the bottom edge of this field. As I look over to my right I can see the sun coming up, just peeking through some of the clouds. It's a lovely golden ball slowly emerging and, with the swans in the field in front, it's a really beautiful sight. This brief moment of tranquillity is interrupted by Paddy starting to pick up his pace again and I just don't trust him this morning so call him back and put his lead on. A few moments later I then spot a fox in the next field so clearly that's what he's been chasing and scenting! We pause for a moment as I try to encourage Paddy to calm himself down but I just know he's going to keep scenting that fox.

All the way down the path next to the lakes Paddy is straining on the lead as there are fox dens scattered all along here. I'm certainly pleased I kept him on the lead otherwise he'd definitely have been off again! In contrast to Paddy being highly strung about the fox, I feel calm as I watch several birds flitting about along here-some blackbirds and a lovely little robin sitting on the fence watching us pass. The sun looks stunning reflecting off the lake here too. At the end of the path we reach the lovely new gate which has been installed. It's an absolute joy to use and I just wish there were more put in like this which are easy for both Paddy and I to get through rather than the styles which have no means of getting a dog through.

Finally, we make our way across the sheep field though, today, there are no sheep. I keep Pads on lead regardless to prevent him eating the sheep poo and piles of potatoes. It seems that sheep like to eat potatoes too as the farmer dumps piles of them out here for them to munch on- who knew?!

WEDNESDAY 22ND DECEMBER 2021
7:30AM : 2 DEGREES C.

Upon opening the curtains this morning I could see it was frosty and it's a lovely, clear, bright, dry day. As we prepare to go out I layer up with my waterproof trousers over my leggings, gloves, coat and head band which should keep me warm. We head out the door and I notice there is a beautiful sunrise this morning. The sky is just a glorious mix of orange, red and yellow, glowing behind all of the houses.

We make our way out of the close and head up past the vets with Paddy almost bouncing on the end of the lead in jubilation that we're going this way. We cross the road and go down past the cemetery and I see the lady who we often see in the mornings when we come this direction. I don't know for certain but my suspicion is that she started these walks in lockdown as it was around that time that we started seeing her and now it seems she walks every morning. She doesn't have a dog; she's just a lady on her own but she always has a fast pace, a small rucksack and I just think it's a really nice thing that she does (one of the good things to come out of lockdown!). I notice an elderly man walking in the cemetery with a scruffy little Terrier and, as we pop into the entrance way to deposit a poo bag in the bin, I hear him singing to himself which puts a smile on my face.

In the close before we enter the fields, there is a house which still has its Christmas lights switched on and it looks lovely. There are twinkling gold fairy lights along the edge of the house and fence as well as gold rope lights edging the path to lead the way up to the front door. There is also a house on the corner which has just two meter square patches of garden at one side and I admire it right through the year (I even nominated it for the 'Lydd in bloom' competition) because they manage to cram it with a mixture of flowers and vegetables. Now they've got some Christmas decorations in there- a silver tree and some well -placed tinsel.

Out in the field I can see that, unfortunately, the best of the sunrise has now passed which is a shame as, out here, with it being so open, it's the perfect viewing point. There is still a nice golden glow and wispy clouds though, with the bright blue sky above. I let Paddy off his lead and we start making our way across the field. The ground is solid following the hard frost we had last night, the mud crunching beneath my feet. I notice that the leaves of the crop which is out here (potatoes I think) have turned silver from the frost, as has the grass.

I'm feeling very happy today, having finished work for the year yesterday and with almost two weeks off ahead of me! It's a very nice feeling knowing I'm not back in work until 4th January. Paddy has now stopped to do some digging- possibly for a mouse- and, whilst he's engrossed in this, I look up ahead and spot what I think is a fox dashing across the next field in the direction we'll soon be heading. So, once Paddy has finished his digging, I'll need to put him on his lead as I just know he'll pick up the scent of that fox and he'll be off! For now though, he's content digging and I appreciate the gentle breeze blowing through the grasses on my left. The grasses look beautiful at the moment- they're all brown, delicate and fluffy, just swaying in the breeze. It is a cold breeze though. In fact, my fingers, despite being in my woolly gloves, are feeling quite cold. However, this is definitely one of my favourite types of weather for dog walking- to be wrapped up warm on a dry day feels very invigorating and it makes getting back home into a warm house even more satisfying.

Surprisingly, Paddy doesn't catch the scent of the fox so, at the end of the next field, I let him off his lead again and he just sniffs his way along the path like usual. We cross the railway line and, in the next field, Paddy has his front feet up on the first step of the bridge, waiting for me to give him the "okay" to cross. In the airport field it's super frosty and I notice that all the lights on the runway are lit so I suspect a plane is due to land soon. As usual, Paddy is just nose to the ground all the way across here, looking for rabbit poo, which I find fairly frustrating so we turn around and start heading back. As we do so, I notice that the sun is starting to come up so we didn't miss the sunrise after all! All of those colours in the sky were clearly just a precursor to the sun emerging. It means I should be able to get a really nice picture of the sunrise over the railway crossing. I stand on the bridge and watch Paddy as he makes his way down the bank and into the river below for a drink. The water level is very low at the moment though, meaning much of the riverbank is exposed and all stodgy (though the frost has hardened it up a bit).

At the railway crossing I ask Paddy to "step up" with his front feet on the railway sleeper and "wait" whilst I get in position to take a photo of him with the sunrise behind. I should probably point out here that this is by no means a main railway line! It's for a goods train which very occasionally goes out to Dungeness and is very slow moving. Thankfully you can hear it coming a mile off too as the driver blasts the horn as it travels along. I take about eight different photos so there should be at least one good one there, especially with Paddy being such a poser! We continue on our way into the next fields and, now that the sun has risen, there's just this incredible golden glow to everything. All of those grasses I noticed as brown on the way now appear a beautiful bronze. Everything just looks magnificent in this light. I always think that this first morning light is particularly special. I look behind me and the sunlight hits me in the face. I think it's going to be a lovely day.

I have come out this morning armed with my secateurs and a carrier bag in my pocket with the intention that we'll now go over to the very small wood (copse?) that we have here. I hope to forage a few bits of greenery to make a Christmas wreath this morning. I usually make it much earlier than this but I've been very busy this year with knitting socks for everyone so any spare moment I've had has been spent on that! I'm very much looking forward to making my wreath though, now that I've finished work.

FRIDAY 31ST DECEMBER 2021
3:45PM : 14 DEGREES C.

It's been unseasonably warm today. So much so, in fact, that it has been declared the warmest New Year's Eve on record! Kris is with us this afternoon and Paddy has decided we're going up to the cricket ground- at each option to go a different route he pulls us towards the cricket ground! Although it's very mild, it's a grey day and fog is starting to descend.

We enter the grassy cricket ground and there is nobody else about so we let Pads off his lead and start walking around the perimeter. Looking across to our left, we realise we can't see the wind farm- it has been shrouded in a blanket of fog. Paddy, meanwhile, has commenced one of his favourite pastimes of eating rabbit poo. We usher him on and make our way down the far edge, parallel to the river. Here, Paddy enjoys looking down the rabbit holes which litter the riverbank.

At the bottom of the field, I'm drawn to a large tree branch above my head. I feel inclined to jump up and hang from it, which I do with a giggle. Kris sees me and encourages me to pull myself up but I can't (upper body strength has never been my strong point!). I jump down and Kris wants to have a go. He clearly has more upper body strength than me and does a few pull ups. We enjoy this moment of play in the playground that nature so often provides for us and continue on our way, the fog thickening as we go. In fact, as we leave the cricket ground, it has become quite dark with the fog fully closing in around us.

We make our way back down the road towards the church which, in this fog and on New Year's Eve, looks and feels incredibly atmospheric with its warm glow emanating through the windows, the lights in the churchyard and the twinkling gold lights adorning the large Christmas tree. I stop to take a photo of Kris and Paddy here but it simply doesn't do it justice. I'm not entirely sure if the warm glow is coming from the lights or from inside me but being here, right now, with Kris and Paddy on our final walk of 2021 feels perfect and I can't think of a better way to end the year.

ABOUT THE AUTHOR

Born in East Sussex, Jo is a country girl whose childhood was filled with dog walks in the countryside and caring for animals on her family's small holding. She has a first class Honours Degree in Applied Animal Behavioural Science and Welfare and now lives in Romney Marsh, Kent with her husband, daughter and Paddy the dog. Jo has a deep appreciation for nature and is content with the simple things in life. Her perfect Sunday includes banana pancakes; time spent pottering in the garden; a long dog walk ending at a pub for a hearty meal and home for a soak in the bath.

ACKNOWLEDGEMENTS

Mum and Dad, thank you for providing me with such a wonderful childhood and teaching me about nature. From bottle-feeding newborn goats in our living room to giving me a patch of garden to grow carrots, you instilled in me a love of animals and the outdoors which will be with me forever.

Kris, your design input for this book is much appreciated, along with the wonderful drawings which feature on various pages. I can't thank you enough for your unwavering support and encouragement in everything I do and for joining me on mad adventures like the Three Peaks Challenge and walking The West Highland Way. I'm grateful that you share my love for the outdoors (and often quiz me on tree names when we're out!) and am excited for the many family adventures we have to come.

Paddy, my four-legged best friend. Thank you for being by my side through everything. Walking in the countryside with you always makes me feel better and I have so many wonderful memories of the adventures we've had together. From bleak winter walks in the pouring rain, to glorious sunny days ambling along country lanes and long runs training for the London Marathon, your cheeky face and boundless enthusiasm for life is infectious. I think we could all do with being a bit more 'Paddy'!

FINAL WORD

Thank you for reading. If you got this far I can only assume you enjoyed it (or you really persevered!). It's been a very long labour of love which spanned the Covid pandemic and lockdowns, my miscarriage and subsequent birth of my wonderful daughter, Evelyn. I'm consequently pretty proud that it has now finally come to fruition, and I've managed to self-publish a book! If you have enjoyed reading it would be pretty cool to have some reviews on Amazon- if you feel so inclined, I'd be very grateful. Here are a few more pictures of my gorgeous Paddy as a thank you.

Jo x